ORCHESTRAL
TECHNIQUE

ORCHESTRAL TECHNIQUE

A MANUAL FOR STUDENTS

BY

GORDON JACOB

PROFESSOR OF COMPOSITION AND
ORCHESTRATION AT THE ROYAL
COLLEGE OF MUSIC

SECOND EDITION

LONDON
OXFORD UNIVERSITY PRESS
NEW YORK   TORONTO

MT
70
J2
1940

Oxford University Press, Ely House, London W. 1

GLASGOW NEW YORK TORONTO MELBOURNE WELLINGTON
CAPE TOWN SALISBURY IBADAN NAIROBI DAR ES SALAAM LUSAKA ADDIS ABABA
BOMBAY CALCUTTA MADRAS KARACHI LAHORE DACCA
KUALA LUMPUR SINGAPORE HONG KONG TOKYO

ISBN 0 19 318201 7

FIRST EDITION 1931
SECOND EDITION 1940
ELEVENTH IMPRESSION 1973

PRINTED IN GREAT BRITAIN AT
THE BOWERING PRESS, PLYMOUTH

PREFACE TO SECOND EDITION

A FEW minor alterations have been made in this edition, and an Appendix has been added which gives further suggestions for exercises in orchestration. Students should be encouraged, however, to use their initiative in seeking out for themselves pieces which seem to them suitable for various orchestral combinations and should not be content to confine themselves to the exercises given in the book.

G. J.

Ewell, Surrey.
June 1940.

PREFACE

THE ability to arrange, for various combinations, music originally written for some other medium, such as the piano or organ, is an important part of the technical equipment of the practical musician. It may fall to his lot to have to arrange music for some church festival, pageant, local concert, folk-dance display, theatricals, amateur and professional, including ballet, and many other occasions foreseen or unforeseen; and though it cannot be too strongly insisted upon that when actually *composing* for orchestra the music must be conceived orchestrally, the writer has found in his own experience of teaching that the study of the art of orchestral transcription confers a double benefit on the student in that it not only teaches him principles of balance, contrast, and colour, but also gives him a truer insight into the underlying structure of music in general by compelling him to translate idioms peculiar to the original medium into those appropriate to the orchestra.

The writer is fully aware that the whole technique of scoring cannot be learned from books alone—experience and common sense being in the end the only teachers, yet he hopes that this book may be of service in pointing out a few of the pitfalls into which the uninitiated invariably fall, and in indicating some of the broad principles of orchestral design.

Lastly, it may possibly be found of use to candidates preparing for examinations in which a knowledge of orchestration is required

G. J.

Ewell, Surrey.
Dec. 1930.

CONTENTS

The following acknowledgements are due for permission to reprint the quotations from copyright works:

To Messrs. JEAN JOBERT, Paris, for the quotations from Debussy's *Toccata.*

To Messrs. AUGENER, LTD., for the quotations from the Augener Edition of Moussorgsky's *Pictures from an Exhibition* and *Ballet de Poussins dans leurs coques* and *Tschaikovsky's Scherzo, Op.* 21, *No.* 6, from the same edition.

CHAPTER I

INTRODUCTORY

THE following are some of the qualifications which the would-be orchestrator should strive to acquire:

1. *A good aural imagination.*

Without the ability to call up to the mind's ear the sound of an orchestral passage from a perusal of the score, all his work will be experimental and unconvincing. Some persons possess this power naturally far more than others, but *it can be acquired* like most other things by means of hard and persistent mental concentration. The first step in the acquisition of this power is to study minutely the scores of works immediately after hearing them, while the aural memory of them is fresh. If this method is seriously pursued (and it demands unremitting attention at concerts and very close study afterwards) it will not be long before the printed score of an unheard work will begin to express itself in actual sound to the mental ear. It is not sufficient alone to follow the score while listening, though it is good to do this, since the music moves on too fast for the eye to take in all the details. The score must be closely studied at leisure after the performance, whether followed during it or not.

2. *Practical common sense.*

Show this by always making your intentions clear in your scores by means of carefully thought-out dynamic markings, bowing of string parts and phrasing of wind; by writing comfortably for your players and avoiding the strain and irritation caused by constant high notes, awkward passages, and too infrequent rests for the wind instruments; by avoiding remote keys—loathed by strings and wind alike. In making orchestral arrangements of music written in remote keys, transpose a semitone up or down according to whether the piece is brilliant or the reverse.

Do not imagine that attention to practical details argues a defective artistic sense. Leave such ideas to romantically-minded novelists. To musicians music is not only an art. It is also a craft, and a complex and difficult one.

3. *A clear and well-ordered style.*

Clarity should be one of the chief ideals of the orchestrator. The texture of the music which you are scoring (whether your own or that of another composer) must be analysed into its component parts, each of which must be carefully balanced or contrasted with the others. Lack of clearness is generally due to a lack of comprehension of the true implications of the music; for example, in transcribing pianoforte music the effect of the sustaining pedal is often not taken into account, the harmonic scheme being thus misinterpreted.

4. *A mind alert for points of interest.*

Seize on any points of interest and bring them out in your score but do not overload it with detail to the extent of 'fussiness' and to the detriment of the main body of the music. Orchestration is a colouristic and decorative art, but the ear should be intrigued, not distracted, by the play of colour. If there is too much going on all the time it will be impossible to make the high-lights or 'peak-points' stand out sufficiently from the rest. Keats's advice to 'load every rift with ore' must not be taken too literally. At the same time monotony and boredom must be most strictly guarded against. Almost all else can be forgiven, but boredom never!

5. *Showmanship and a sense of the dramatic.*

Do not be afraid of being 'effective', but shun effect merely for effect's sake. Whatever the mood of the piece of music you are scoring, your orchestration should emphasize and enhance it. This is the true meaning of effectiveness or of 'putting it over', as they say in the theatre. The abuse of effect shows itself when inappropriate means are used simply to show off one's imagined skill and knowledge of the orchestra. In such cases orchestration descends to the level of a conjuring trick which depends for its effect on a series of shocks and surprises. The object of orchestration is not to show how clever one is—that is of no interest to any one—but to present the music in its clearest and most appropriate orchestral form.

．　　．　　．　　．　　．　　．　　．　　．　　．

The full orchestra consists of four departments—strings, woodwind, brass, and percussion. The string department is made up of 1st violins,

2nd violins, violas, violoncellos, and double basses. In a large orchestra the players in each group would number approximately as follows: 16, 14, 10, 10, 8. The woodwind consists normally of two each of the following: flutes, oboes, clarinets, and bassoons. In the 'Wagnerian' orchestra triple woodwind is used, giving the following arrangement:

2 flutes+3rd flute or piccolo.
2 oboes+3rd oboe or cor anglais.
2 clarinets+3rd clarinet or bass clarinet.
2 bassoons+3rd bassoon or double bassoon.

Some very fully scored modern symphonic and operatic works employ quadruple woodwind, such exotics as the bass flute and heckelphone sometimes being added to the flute and oboe group respectively. The use of 4 bassoons is not uncommon in modern French scores, the 4th player alternating with double bassoon. It must be remembered that, whereas in the string department several players play the same part, in the other departments each individual instrument has its own separate part. 'Doubling,' however, as we shall see later, is of very frequent occurrence in the wind and brass departments.

The brass consists of the following:

2 trumpets, 4 horns, 2 tenor trombones, 1 bass trombone, and 1 tuba (bass tuba).

Occasionally 3, 4, or even 5 trumpets, 6 or 8 horns, and tenor as well as bass tuba are used. It is very rare indeed to find more than 3 trombones employed.

The percussion consists of timpani (or kettledrums), bass drum, cymbals, side-drum, triangle, tambourine, gong, castanets, xylophone, &c., &c., according to taste. Percussion players should be able to play all the percussion instruments. It is therefore more practical and economical to have one player for timpani only, and one, or at most two players for whatever other percussion instruments are required, percussion players being accustomed to change quite rapidly from one instrument to another.

The harp, celesta, and pianoforte cannot be classified under any of the above departmental headings. Of these three the harp is now a regular member of the orchestra, the others being sometimes used for special effects.

The Full Score is arranged in the following order, woodwind being placed at the head of the score, then brass, then percussion, then harp, &c., and the strings at the bottom. Each pair of wind and brass players is allotted one stave in the score, which stands thus:

Flutes I and II. (If flute II is also needed for piccolo his part is written on an extra stave)
(Flute III or piccolo)
Oboes I and II
(Oboe III or cor anglais)
Clarinets I and II
(Clarinet III or bass clarinet)
Bassoons I and II
(Bassoon III or double bassoon)
Horns I and II
Horns III and IV
Trumpets I and II

Tenor trombones I and II
Bass trombone
Tuba
Timpani
Other percussion
(Celesta)
(Piano)
Harp
Violin I
Violin II
Viola
Violoncello
Double bass

To facilitate score-reading we give below the English, Italian, French, and German names for the instruments, arranged in parallel columns:

English.	Italian.	French.	German.
Flute	Flauto	Flûte	Flöte
Piccolo	Flauto Piccolo	Petite Flûte	Kleine Flöte
Oboe (or Hautboy)	Oboe	Hautbois	Hoboe
Cor Anglais (or English Horn)	Corno Inglese	Cor Anglais	Englisches Horn
Clarinet	Clarinetto	Clarinette	Klarinette
Bass Clarinet	Clarinetto Basso	Clarinette basse	Bassklarinette
Bassoon	Fagotto	Basson	Fagott
Double Bassoon	Contrafagotto	Contre-Basson	Kontrafagott
Horn	Corno	Cor	Horn
Trumpet	Tromba	Trompette	Trompete
Trombone	Trombone	Trombone	Posaune

English.	Italian.	French.	German.
Tuba	Tuba	Tuba	Tuba
Timpani (or Kettledrums)	Timpani	Timbales	Pauken
Bass Drum	Gran Cassa	Grosse Caisse	Grosse Trommel
Cymbals	Piatti or Cinelli	Cymbales	Becken
Side-drum	Tamburo militare	Tambour militaire	Kleine Trommel
Triangle	Triangolo	Triangle	Triangel
Tambourine	Tamburino	Tambour de Basque	Schellentrommel
Tenor Drum	Tamburo rullante	Caisse roulante	Rührtrommel
Gong	Tam-tam	Tam-tam	Tam-tam
Glockenspiel	Campanetta	Carillon	Glockenspiel
Xylophone	Zilafone	Xylophone	Xylophon
Celesta	Celesta	Céleste	Celeste
Bells	Campanelle	Cloches	Glocken
Harp	Arpa	Harpe	Harfe
Violin	Violino	Violon	Violine
Viola	Viola	Alto	Bratsche
Violoncello	Violoncello	Violoncelle	Violoncell
Double Bass	Contrabasso	Contre basse	Kontrabass

In writing the score, the names of the instruments as well as the proper clefs and key-signatures must appear on the first page. After that it will be necessary only to place clefs and signatures on each left-hand page. The bar-lines should not be ruled continuously down the page, but should be ruled with gaps between the woodwind, brass, percussion, and string groups. This makes the score much easier to read.

In the following chapters each orchestral group is studied separately before being combined with the others. The strings, forming as they do the foundation of the orchestra, have the first claim on our attention, and we may now proceed without further preliminaries to our consideration of the string orchestra.

CHAPTER II

THE STRING ORCHESTRA

THE string orchestra, as we have said, consists of all the members of the violin family—violins, divided into firsts and seconds, violas, violoncellos, and double basses.

We shall see later that it is sometimes necessary further to subdivide these groups in music of a complex nature, but the above arrangement is the normal one and departures from it should be as infrequent as is compatible with the adequate presentation of the music.

The strings provide us with the most expressive and appealing medium (with perhaps the exception of the human voice) that exists in the whole range of music. A good string orchestra can attain a degree of pianissimo which amounts to little more than an attenuated whisper, and is also capable of a robust and solid fortissimo which is almost 'brassy' in its effect. Between these limits any degree of nuance is practicable. Still further varieties and contrasts of tone are available by such mechanical means as the mute (*sordino*), the plucking (*pizzicato*), instead of bowing, of the strings, the ponticello tremolo in which a most eerie effect is produced by bowing the strings nearer to the bridge than the normal position, the col legno (a very rare effect) in which the strings are struck with the back of the bow, giving a sound like the rattle of dry sticks, &c., &c.

If, as we are assuming, good professional players are available, we can take the following as safe working compasses for the various instruments:

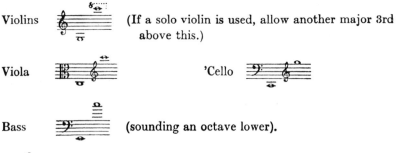

Violins   (If a solo violin is used, allow another major 3rd above this.)

Viola   'Cello

Bass   (sounding an octave lower).

6

Few occasions, however, will present themselves for using the extreme upward limits of compass.

Very high altitudes can also be attained by the employment of natural and artificial harmonics, but here again the use of these is the exception rather than the rule, and a good deal of practical knowledge of string technique is required for their safe and appropriate use. Those who wish to avail themselves of all the different kinds of harmonics possible will find the information they require in the larger text books of orchestration. The student will also find Robjohn's short treatise, *Violin Technique* (Oxford Musical Essays), stimulating and helpful in connexion with string writing. We are more concerned here with what might be called the roast beef of scoring than with the confectionery.

The normal lay-out of the string orchestra is in four-part harmony, the double bass either doubling the 'cellos, or being silent. We would here stress the importance of giving plenty of rests to the double basses. Few things are more fatiguing to the ear than the incessant doubling of the bass at the octave below, in season and out of season. No organist in his senses would use sixteen-foot tone throughout an extended work, so why should the orchestrator? We would advise the beginner never to write his 'cello and bass parts on the same staff: if he does, he will almost surely fall into the error of over-using the double bass, his mind's ear, which acts through his eye, being almost certain to fail to register the lower octave. Moreover, we do not wish to give the impression that the 'cello and bass always work in double harness: on the contrary, they can be used independently to a quite large extent, though discretion and careful thought are very necessary in this matter, since the basses when used alone tend to sound rather dry, and if their part lies low and is far removed in pitch from the rest of the harmony it is too indeterminate in pitch to give satisfactory support unless it consists of a sustained or better (since the bow is short) a reiterated pedal note. In a quiet harmonic passage, however, in which the bass does not lie extremely low. the double basses may be entrusted with the lowest part. Always think how the passage would *look* if the bass were written at its true pitch instead of an octave higher. In a five-part polyphonic passage in which an independent 'cello part is necessary, it is always better to divide the 'cellos, and to give the lowest part to the second half of the 'cellos either

7

in actual unison (pitch permitting) or in the octave above the double basses.

The following extract from the Fugue in C♯ minor from Book I of the '48' illustrates this point. It should be compared with the original (bars 73-82).

Ex. I

Fugue in C♯ minor

The 2nd 'cellos here play in *unison* with the double basses for the first
six bars, and after that in the octave above, the double basses being more
effective if kept in the lower octave. The objection to this arrangement
is that only half the 'cellos are available for the important entries in the
second and ninth bars, which are thus considerably weakened. For this
reason we have marked the 2nd 'cello part to be played by one desk only
(i.e. two players) if the orchestra is large, and one player only if it is small.
This would be quite sufficient to lend distinctness to the double-bass
part, and would leave a large proportion of the 'cellos free to play the
1st 'cello part.

In our next example, which consists of the last two bars of the
Prelude in B♭ minor from Book I of the '48' a different lay-out will
be seen.

Ex. II

Here, if the 'cellos are equally divided, the balance will be satisfactory
because of the powerful and penetrating tone of the 1st 'cellos on their
top string. This arrangement also has the advantage of placing the
violas in their most effective and characteristic register, namely on their
C string. Another point to be noted in this connexion is that if the
dynamic range of a passage does not exceed *mf*, the balance, upset by the
division of one or more departments of the strings, can be restored by

9

means of suitable expression-marks. For instance, if, in Ex. I, the passage were desired to be played *mf* instead of *ff*, the 'cellos could be equally divided if the 1st 'cello parts were marked *f* while all the other parts were marked *mf*.

In *f* and *ff* passages the weakest part needs strengthening, if numbers permit, in the way indicated above (i.e. by unequal division).

Chords of two, three, and four notes are often written for violin, viola, and 'cello, but great care has to be exercised in their use to avoid technical difficulties. The easiest chords of two notes are, of course, those of which one note is an open string, but by 'double-stopping', i.e. stopping two notes on adjacent strings, any of the following may be safely written:

Major or minor 3rds up to

Perfect or augmented 4ths up to

Perfect, augmented, and diminished 5ths up to

Major or minor 6ths up to

Major and minor 7ths up to
(diminished 7ths same as major 6ths)

Octaves up to

10

Major and minor 2nds are perhaps best avoided except when an open string can be used, e.g.:

(transpose a fifth, or a ninth higher for the other strings).

Note that in the above example the E♭ and E♮ are played on the G string, the D string remaining open.

It is most important to remember that no double-stop can be played of which the higher note is lower than , since this would require both notes to be stopped on the same string simultaneously.

With regard to three-note chords it will be safest for the student who has no practical knowledge of string-technique to confine himself almost entirely to those which contain at least one open string. These, as well as being the easiest are also the most powerful and effective, but chords consisting of combinations of 5ths and 6ths such as the following are easy and sonorous:

(1) Chromatically from ⟶ to

(2) Chromatically from ⟶ to

(3) Chromatically from ⟶ to

The above are all available in the minor form also, with the exception of

and

Major and minor chords of *four* notes arranged thus, chromatically from to are all possible and effective.

All the above chords, if transposed a fifth lower, are suitable for the viola, and, if transposed an octave and a fifth lower, for the 'cello also.

Owing to the curvature of the bridge, the top two notes only of a three or four-part chord can be sustained. If this effect is required, write thus:

Three and four-part chords are effective only in *f* and *ff*, and are best used in the orchestra when a series of emphatic detached chords is desired.

Ex. III   Beethoven — Sonata in C minor (Pathétique)

All the chords in this example are easy and effective. Note that the actual spacing of the pianoforte chords is not adhered to in the arrangement. The first chord would sound lamentably thin if laid out as it stands in the original, and the last two would be hopelessly thick and stodgy if literally transcribed. On the pianoforte such chords have a fine percussive effect.

12

On strings, and indeed on any orchestral combination, they would sound dull and muddy to a degree.

We might thus formulate two rules such as the following:

(i) When transcribing a passage from pianoforte score in which the two hands are spaced far apart, fill in the gap in your arrangement.

(ii) When thick low-placed chords occur in the left hand part, rearrange them with a clear octave at the bottom of the chords.

The secret of effective arrangement is in adapting the idiom of your original to that of your instrumental medium. A good arrangement should sound as though it were an original conception, and not an arrangement at all. In short, it is often necessary to alter the letter of the original in order to preserve its spirit.

The following examples should give hints as to how this result may be obtained.

Ex. IV
Beethoven, Op. 14, No. 2

Vln. I
Vln. II
Vla.
Vcl.
C.B.

Ex. IV shows the treatment of a simple 'Alberti bass'. It will be seen that the harmonic scheme of the original has been strictly adhered to, though it has been considerably amplified. The slurs in the left-hand part indicate a smooth sustained bass. This is provided by the 'cello in the arrangement. The double bass *pizzicato* provides the two bass notes in each bar, required by the original, and also supplies lightness, rhythm, and 'spring' to the whole texture.

Ex. V demands extremely smooth treatment. In our arrangement no amplifications have been made, the arpeggios being sufficiently wide-spread to bridge the gap between melody and bass. The way in which

the arpeggio-figure has been divided between 2nd violin and viola prevents harmonic thinness and ensures smoothness. Observe the slight modification rendered necessary in bar 6 owing to the lack of the low B on the viola, and how in the same bar, the doubling of the 7th in the dominant 7th is avoided by the return of the viola to D♯ on the third beat.

Ex. VI   Moussorgsky — Pictures from an Exhibition, No. 7, 'Limoges'

The first four bars of Ex. VI would appear simple enough to arrange. It is only when the fifth bar is reached that problems arise. An uncomfort-able inner part appears, and at the same time an awkward leap across the strings between the last semiquaver of bar 4 and the first of bar 5 in the top part gives us pause. We will try to overcome both these obstacles together. It would obviously be the worst of craftsmanship to score the first four bars as they stand for the violins and viola and at the fifth bar to weaken one of the parts by division. At the same time the inner part lies too high for it to be entrusted to the 'cellos without probable results

16

of the most devastating nature. Let us rather ask ourselves how we would score bar 5 if it stood alone apart from its context, and adapt the first four bars to this arrangement so as to lead naturally into it. The most obvious arrangement of bar 5 is that shown in our example—the top part to the 1st violins, the next lower to the 2nd violins, and the repeated chords below to the violas *divisi*. We will therefore allot the repeated chords throughout to violas *divisi*. By doing this we have also solved the problem of the awkward leap referred to above; for, by giving the top line to the 2nd violins in the first four bars all technical difficulties are avoided, and, in addition, force and verve are given to the sforzando on the first beat of bar 5, and greater point and conviction are gained for the abrupt change of key.

Note the effect of the *pizzicato* chord for 1st violins and 'cellos at the beginning, and that the directions 'arco, unis.', have not been omitted from the 1st violin part on its re-entrance. Further note that in bar 3, viola part, the flat sign is placed before the C when it first appears in the lower part as well as at its first appearance in the upper part. In the band-parts *divisi* passages are usually written on two staves; it is therefore necessary to insert all accidentals in both the upper and lower factors of the *divisi*.

In Ex. VII we have a 'broken chord' passage which demands strong vigorous treatment. It should be obvious that what is really implied

Ex. VII   Grieg—Sonata in E minor

here is the rapid repetition of the complete chords, which would be impossible on the pianoforte at the required speed. Our arrangement is a simple translation of pianoforte language into that of strings. Note the filling in of the middle of the harmony by the violas, which gives solidity to the structure. The effect of this passage should be brilliant and exciting, and its brilliance would be enhanced in no small degree by the presence of the open E string of the 2nd violins.

Ex. VIII   Grieg—Sonata in E minor

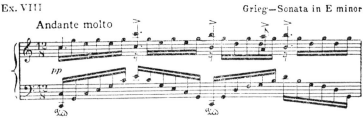

cantabile

Vln. I (div.)

Vln. II (div.)

Vla. (div.)

Vcl. (div.)

C. B. (1 desk)

Example VIII requires rather more elaborate treatment. In our arrangement the arpeggios in the left-hand part of the original are divided between the 1st violas and 1st 'cellos. The 2nd violins (*divisi*) play the semiquaver figure in the right-hand part an octave apart and in contrary motion. The 2nd violas fill in the middle of the harmony by means of very easy double-stops. The 2nd 'cellos sustain the bass, doubled by one desk of double basses *pizzicato*. The melody is given to the 1st violins (also *divisi*) in octaves. At first sight this arrangement might possibly appear needlessly elaborate, but it would be difficult to obtain

19

in any other way a full body of tone corresponding to that provided by the sustaining pedal of the pianoforte. Were the passage to be literally transcribed, with the melody in octaves on the 1st violins and violas, the semiquaver figures in the right-hand to the second violins and the arpeggios in the left-hand to the 'cellos, the intentions of the composer would be most inadequately represented. The effect of the sustaining pedal must always be most carefully taken into consideration when transcribing pianoforte music.

It would be possible to go on multiplying instances of the adaptation of the pianoforte idiom to that of the string orchestra, but space is limited, and the above examples will have to suffice. The following passages, taken from well-known or easily obtainable pianoforte music, are suggested as exercises in scoring for string orchestra.

1. Bach, 12 Short Preludes (Augener), No. 9 in F.
   6 Short Preludes (Augener), No. 1 in C, and No. 4 in D.
   (In scoring these the semiquaver figures should be divided between the various string-parts, and a little unobtrusive 'filling up' is advisable at times where the texture becomes thin.)

2. Beethoven, Sonata in B flat, Op. 22. First movement (as far as the first double-bar only). In bar 26 &c. the left-hand figure should be

   rendered thus: 🎵 etc.

   Rearrangement and filling-in are necessary in bars 4–7.

3. Beethoven, Sonata in G minor, Op. 49, No. 1. (The complete work.)

4. Brahms, 'Variations on a Hungarian Song,' Op. 21, No. 2. (Omitting Vars. 12 and 13.) (Breitkopf and Härtel.)

5. Grieg, Sonata in E minor, 1st movement.

CHAPTER III

WOODWIND AND HORNS

THE normal orchestral woodwind group consists of two each of the following: flutes, oboes, clarinets, and bassoons. In small and incomplete orchestras, however, such combinations as the following are often to be found:

(*a*) 1 fl. 1 ob. 1 clar. 1 bassoon.
(*b*) 1 fl. 1 ob. 2 clar. 1 bassoon.
(*c*) 2 fl. 1 ob. 2 clar. 1 bassoon.
(*d*) 1 fl. 1 clar.

In a small orchestra two oboes would be too penetrating and reedy in tone, and two bassoons too thick.

The horns, though they properly belong to the brass group, are so frequently used as part of the woodwind ensemble that we feel bound to include them in our consideration of this orchestral group. It is rare to find a single horn in a small orchestra. They nearly always hunt in couples, so one expects to find either no horns at all or two horns. In the full orchestra four horns (or, more accurately, two pairs of horns) are now always to be found.

Let us first briefly consider each of these instruments in turn.

1. *The Flute.*

The compass of this instrument is

The top two semitones, B♮ and C are, however, rather difficult to produce and should only be used at the end of an upward-rushing *ff* scale.

The low register of the flute, by which we mean the notes between and

including   is very rich and beautiful and has been much

exploited by latter-day composers, especially those of the French school. In spite of its richness and apparent power when heard absolutely alone, solo passages in this register are very easily obscured by other instruments and must therefore be very lightly accompanied. These low notes (especially when played by two or three flutes in unison) bear a striking resemblance to those of a distant trumpet and have been known to deceive even a practised ear, temporarily off its guard, into thinking that a trumpet is actually playing. The magical 'pagan' effect of the flute in this part of its compass is nowhere better demonstrated than in

Debussy's 'L'après-midi d'un faune'. From the flute is

eminently suited to quiet melodic work, florid or otherwise. Here again the accompaniment must be light in texture or the flute will not stand

out clearly from its background. From ♯ upwards the flute

possesses a clear bright tone and considerable penetrating power. Its high register gives brilliance and point when doubling at the octave phrases allotted to other wind instruments or to the violins. The flute is an extremely agile instrument both in scale and arpeggio work, staccato and legato (but in its low register the staccato is difficult of clear articulation and is safer avoided) and is capable of extremely rapid repetition of a single note in the medium and upper registers.

The following two shakes are impossible on the flute.

All others are playable except those which lie at the extreme top end of

the compass (say above ♯ including the shake on G and A♮).

2. *The Oboe.*

Compass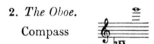

This is a double-reed instrument which possesses a penetrating, rather nasal tone which, however, is capable of great musical expression in the

hands of a sensitive artist. From ♯ upwards its tone becomes thin

and rather unsatisfactory, the flute being far preferable at that altitude.

It is essentially a melodic instrument and, though holding-notes in music of light calibre are charming in effect (especially from

or thereabouts with the exception of C*) it cannot efface itself sufficiently to carry out the menial task of 'filling in notes of the harmony' in block-writing. That is the reason why only one oboe is usually found in small orchestras. In the full orchestra the richness of the general ensemble of course reduces the prominence of the oboe tone.

As a solo instrument it is admirable for the expression of poignant melodies or short expressive phrases, and is, of course, a *sine qua non* in music of a pastoral nature. It is also capable of considerable agility and can take a delightful part in 'woodwind dialogues' in which little phrases are tossed about and discussed in turn by the different woodwind voices.

Its best range for solos is

The staccato of the oboe is very telling, and fairly rapid reiteration is within its powers. The bottom notes have often been maligned in text-books, but, as a matter of fact, they are rich and luscious and admirable when the dynamic force is *mf* or more. These notes, however, should be used sparingly as they soon pall on the ear.

Do not write shakes above ⟨notation⟩ All others are possible, but ⟨notation⟩ is to be avoided.

One more word—Have mercy on the player and give him plenty of rests. The oboe is fatiguing to play, and breathing spaces are essential.

3. *The Clarinet* (single-reed instrument).

Two clarinets are in use at the present day, in B♭ and A.

This means that when the player plays C on his B♭ instrument, it sounds B♭. When he plays C on his A instrument it sounds A. Hence the part for a B♭ clarinet is written a tone higher than the key of the piece, and that for an A clarinet a minor 3rd higher. Thus, however flat or sharp the key of the piece may be, the arranger is able to see to it that his

* This exception does not apply to first-rate players.

23

clarinets are playing in no key with a greater number of flats or sharps than three.

For instance if the piece is in E♭ the B♭ clarinet will be chosen and will play in the key of F; if the piece is in D♭ the key of the B♭ clarinet part will be E♭, and so on. If the key of the piece is D, the A clarinet is chosen, which will be in F, (the key a minor 3rd higher). If the key of the piece is B, the A clarinet part will be in D, and so on.

Therefore in flat keys write for the B♭ clarinet, and in sharp keys for the A.* Sometimes of course a section of a work may be in a key remote from that of the main body of the piece. In that case do not change from B♭ to A or vice versa for the offending section, unless the clarinet is to have an important solo passage during its course. Players do not like setting down an instrument that has just become nicely warmed up, and taking up a cold one unless there is a very good reason for it. The worldly-wise orchestrator will rather see to it that there is *not* an important clarinet part in the aforesaid section. In other words he will give the tune to somebody else!

There is no discernible difference in quality between the timbre of the B♭ and A clarinet, though performers seem to prefer the A instrument on the whole. The choice between them should thus rest entirely on simplicity of key—the piece as a whole with all its modulations and sectional key-changes being taken into consideration. The fingering and general technique of both clarinets are precisely the same, as is also their written

compass:

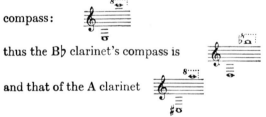

thus the B♭ clarinet's compass is

and that of the A clarinet

The treble clef is always used even for the bottom notes.

The bottom octave of the clarinet compass (which is known as the

* But remote keys, e.g. G♭ and C♯ must be regarded as their enharmonic equivalents i.e. F♯ and D♭, the A clarinet being used for the former and the B♭ for the latter.

24

chalumeau register) is extremely characteristic and unlike any sound produced by any other instrument. It is rich and oily, hollow and rather sinister, especially when a note is attacked *sforzando*, or a held note swells and dies away. The tone of the clarinet in this register must be heard and retained in the mind. It cannot be adequately described.

From  the tone is dull and lifeless, and no important solo-

work revolving round these notes should be given to the clarinet. Incidentally this also happens to be the most difficult part of the instruments' compass from the point of view of fingering. Of course arpeggios and passage-work generally can freely *pass through* this part of the compass; it is only when a passage turns and returns on itself within these narrow limits that it becomes both really awkward for the player and uninteresting in sound. The rest of the clarinet's compass is clear and uniform, and it is a perfect solo instrument if not taken too high. The writer is aware that first-rate players can produce a beautifully pure

pianissimo up to   (*written* note), but such players do not grow

on every bush, and   may be taken as about the upward limit for

safety in solo work. The top notes are apt to be 'screamy' and too shrill for anything but rather grotesque effects.

The clarinet is of great agility, and passages based on arpeggios are very much in its character. It is, however, equally good in scale passages, legato, and staccato, in wide leaps, in rapid changes from *p* to *f* and it is capable of more varied and more subtle tonal nuance than is any other wind instrument. Passages for two clarinets in 3rds or 6ths are in the stock-in-trade of every orchestrator and are always of excellent effect.

Avoid these shakes

4. *The Bassoon* (double-reed instrument).

This instrument is usually designated in scores by the abbreviation *Fag.*, its Italian name being *Fagotto*.

Its part is non-transposing and it possesses a compass of three octaves:

Higher notes can be obtained (e.g. at the opening of Stravinsky's 'Sacre du Printemps', where top C's and D's are used with extraordinary and eerie effect in the unaccompanied passage for solo bassoon with which that masterpiece begins) but the B♭ given is a safe limit for the average player. The bass clef is used for the lower parts of the compass, the tenor for the higher.

The natural function of the bassoon is to provide the bass of the woodwind group, but it is frequently used as a melodic instrument, both 'solo' and when doubled in the upper octave by another wind instrument or sometimes by the violins. Mozart has shown us on many occasions in his scores how delightful a melodic phrase can sound when given to bassoon and flute at two octaves distance. Two bassoons and two clarinets blend admirably in four-part harmony, and two bassoons and two horns used *pp* or *p* are a good substitute for four horns. The bassoon also agrees well with its double-reed cousin the oboe, and the unison of high bassoon and low flute is exceedingly attractive. This instrument is thus seen to be a splendid complement to the other members of the woodwind fraternity.

It has considerable agility, and its powers of dry staccato have been so much exploited that this form of musical humour has quite lost its savour nowadays. This splendid instrument, once miscalled the 'clown of the orchestra' is worthy of better labels. Its lowest octave is rich reedy and powerful and its middle and upper register have a fine slightly throaty quality well suited to dignified and expressive solos.

Avoid all shakes below ⟨notation⟩ and those on D♭, E♭, G♭, in all octaves,

as well as that on the top A ⟨notation⟩

The following woodwind instruments, in addition to those described above are often used in the full orchestra. They are, however, in the nature of luxuries (with the exception of the piccolo). These are the piccolo, cor anglais (or English horn), bass clarinet, and double bassoon (contrafagotto).

5. *The Piccolo.*

This is a miniature flute with written compass (sounding an octave higher).

It is very shrill and piercing in its top register, which thus requires the support of a large orchestral mass. Its bottom octave is too weak for ordinary use, though it is attractive when extremely lightly accompanied. The piccolo is very rarely used completely 'solo', but is much used to double other woodwind instruments at the octave or double octave above. It is, if possible, even more agile than the flute. The piccolo is played by the 2nd flautist (or in large orchestras by the 3rd) who plays flute or piccolo as required. The change from flute to piccolo or vice versa occupies only a few seconds.

6. *The Cor Anglais.*

This is a large oboe with written compass (sounding a fifth lower *i.e.*)

It is a very beautiful instrument, chiefly used for solo work where a melancholy and expressive tone-quality is appropriate. It is at its best and most characteristic in its bottom octave-and-a-half. The 2nd oboe player is sometimes called upon to play cor anglais, but in large orchestras a cor anglais is present in addition to the two oboes. It can be used as an inner voice in the woodwind ensemble, but tends to be obtrusive. It is essentially a solo instrument. Examples of its use in this way are to be found in 'Tristan' (opening of Act III), New World Symphony (slow movement), Sibelius' 'Swan of Tuonela', Berlioz's 'Carnaval Romain' Overture, Vaughan Williams' London Symphony (opening of slow movement). It also doubles violas or 'cellos with good effect and blends well with low or lowish clarinets.

7. *The Bass Clarinet.*

This is a large clarinet, standing an octave below the B flat clarinet. Its part is written in the treble clef a 9th higher than the sounded notes.

Written Compass sounding

Most bass clarinets have the low E♭, indicated by the black note. There is no bass clarinet in A.* The bass clarinet forms a solid bass for the woodwind group, often being placed below the bassoons. Its bottom octave and a half is extremely rich, woody, and quite unlike anything else. It is often given solo passages to play, and its tone is so intrinsically striking that entirely unaccompanied phrases are not infrequently allotted to it. Its richness and flexibility make it extremely useful in doubling and giving clearness to important melodic bass parts played by 'cellos, double basses, &c. Its upper register lacks character and individuality when heard alone, but is often useful in doubling other instruments in an important middle part. A bass clarinet is used in large orchestras in addition to the two ordinary clarinets, and occasionally the 2nd clarinet in smaller orchestras is called upon to change to bass clarinet. This is rare and risky, however, as all clarinet players do not possess a bass clarinet, which is a very expensive instrument. Examples of its use in various ways are to be found in 'Tristan' and 'Parsifal' (many unaccompanied recitative-like passages), Tschaikowsky's 'Danse de la Fée-Dragée' from the 'Casse-Noisette' Suite (very few notes, but marvellously effective), Elgar's Symphony No. 2 (endless examples of bass clarinet doublings), Stravinsky's 'Petrouchka' (in the 1st scene where it is used with two ordinary clarinets during the extraordinarily realistic hurdy-gurdy episode, and in the Moor's scene later on with grotesquely sinister effect).

8. *The Double Bassoon.*

This, as its name indicates, is a large bassoon. It corresponds, in the woodwind department, to the double basses in the string group and, like theirs, its part is written an octave higher than it sounds.

* Wagner and others wrote for Bass Clarinet in A, but such parts are played on the B♭ instrument.

Written compass,  sounding

The function of the double bassoon is to add weight to the bass. It is incapable of much agility, and its part should be as simple as possible. Its high notes are not of good quality. The double bassoon should only be used, as a general rule, in fully scored passages. Its tone is obtrusive and difficult to subdue. It is excellent as a bass-strengthener, however, in dynamic ranges of *mf* and upwards. It should always be used with definite intention—never mechanically added to the ensemble without consciously imagining its effect. Of course, in very full and loud tuttis it can be used freely. *But write a simple part for it* and do not keep it going long without rests.

9. *The Horn.*

The whole mechanism and technique of this instrument differs absolutely from those of the woodwind. The tone is produced by the action of the player's lips (technically known as 'embouchure') and wind pressure operating on a small conical mouthpiece, and setting the air in the instrument in vibration. It is not within the scope of this book to enter into a detailed explanation of the technique of the horn, but the fact should be firmly grasped that it is based on the possibility of producing by means of varying embouchure the upper partials of the harmonic series derived from a fundamental note, the pitch of which depends on the length of the tube. In order to produce notes outside the rather restricted number determined by the harmonic series it is therefore necessary to alter the pitch of the fundamental. The horn is fitted with three valves or pistons and it is the function of these valves to lower the pitch of the instrument in varying degrees by opening up fresh lengths of tube. By using the valves separately and in combination a sufficient number of harmonic series is obtained to give the instrument a chromatic compass.

The following notes of the harmonic series are obtainable from a fundamental C.

* Notes of uncertain intonation

29

Lower the fundamental, say a semitone, by introducing a fresh length of tube, and the whole series is lowered a semitone; lengthen the tube still more and the series is lowered a tone, and so on. Each valve or combination of valves, therefore, produces not a single note but a whole series of possible notes, the one required at any moment being selected and coaxed out by the player, who must therefore 'feel' the required note before he actually produces it. After a time this ability becomes as instinctive as is the power of singing or whistling a note of any pitch desired, but it should be obvious that horn parts should keep to 'vocal' intervals or stepwise movement as far as possible.

On the horn, by the way, the actual fundamental note of each series cannot be produced; each series therefore begins with the first harmonic, i.e. the octave from the fundamental.

Before the invention and perfection of valves, horns in all keys were used owing to the narrow range of notes available on the natural horn. Their parts were always written in the key of C, a 'crook' or detachable length of curved tube determining the key in which the instrument was set. Thus in scores of the classical period we find horns in C, D, E♭, E, F, &c., &c., and horn parts of a necessarily very simple and diatonic character, and all *written* in the key of C but *sounding* in the key of the piece.

For instance

Horns in D

whereas the same passage for horns in E♭ would sound

and so on through all the keys. The horn in C sounded an octave lower than the written note.

Now that all this complication is unnecessary owing to the introduction of valves, one horn is universally used. This is the HORN IN F. The passage given above would of course sound if played on F horns. We thus see that horn parts have to be written a fifth higher than the pitch required.

The bass clef is used for the lowest parts of the horn's compass, which is a wide one, extending from

The extreme notes at both ends of the compass are difficult to produce, and the following is the normal written working compass of the horn.

Higher notes may be reached in *ff* by good symphony-orchestra players, and are often found in big modern scores, but they are extremely risky for the average player and cause physical discomfort both to him and his audience.

Do not write *p* or *pp* passages above

Below

write only long holding notes. Moving parts low down in the horn's compass are ineffective.

Formerly, notes written in the bass clef were written a fourth lower than the required pitch instead of a fifth higher. This practice has no foundation in common sense, and is disappearing. The student is advised to write a fifth higher than the required note whether in treble or bass clef. Until the old system entirely dies out, however, some verbal indication of this should be given in the horn parts.*

Horn parts are usually written, as in the old pre-valve days, without key-signature, the necessary accidentals being added. The use of key-signatures is, however, gaining ground and has the advantage of giving the player a surer sense of the tonality of the piece. The writer of this

* e.g. " New notation for bass clef."

book has to confess that so far he has been so hide-bound by tradition that he has not yet brought himself to write key-signatures for the horns, but he admits that the only argument in favour of this is that the lack of signature acts as a guide to the conductor's eye in spotting the horn parts in the score, but he advises those less trammelled by convention than himself to adopt the use of key signatures for both horns and trumpets!

The horn is a profoundly expressive instrument when used for quiet, simple, melodic utterances in its medium register, roughly, say

One has only to recall such beautiful horn solos as that in the Andante of Tschaikovsky's 5th Symphony, and Mendelssohn's Nocturne from the *Midsummer Nights' Dream* music, to mention but two examples, to realize this. It is also capable of the most savage attack when roused, the stridency of which is enhanced (though the power actually reduced) by 'stopping' the bell with the hand or a metal mute and blowing hard. The former effect, known as the 'cuivré' is indicated by a cross, thus

It should be reserved for moments of dramatic intensity or terror. When played f or $f\!f$ in the ordinary way (unmuted) the tone is broad, sonorous, and noble.

For very romantic distant or 'echo' effects the muted horn blown very softly is admirable. No other orchestral sound has quite the same feeling as of 'magic casements opening . . .'

Quiet holding notes and fairly stationary filling-in parts constitute the main part of the duty of the horns, as any score will show, but we shall see later on that they are also very useful in doubling other instruments when it is desired to give 'body' and prominence to a broad melodic line in the tenor register. Repeated notes, both in groups of twos and threes, are a characteristic feature of horn writing, and though passages requiring considerable agility are to be found in most modern scores they are usually well and safely doubled by other instruments, as they are apt to sound woolly and ill-defined in shape if left to the horns alone. Shakes are possible if confined to notes within the treble staff, but opportunities for their appropriate use are very rare and the inexperienced orchestrator is advised to keep his horn parts in general as simple as possible, and to avoid wide and 'unvocal' leaps.

The first horn should rarely go below

and the second should rarely be taken above

The high and low notes require different embouchures. This rule is not a rigid one however, especially in unison passages for the two horns.

EXERCISES

1. Write melodies and cadenzas suitable for (a) the flute, (b) the oboe, (c) the bassoon, (d) the cor anglais.

2. Transpose the following passages with proper key-signatures for (a) B♭ clarinet, (b) A clarinet, (c) F horn, (d) Bass clarinet.

8. Write melodies and cadenzas suitable for (a) the clarinet, (b) the horn.

CHAPTER IV

WOODWIND AND HORNS (*cont.*)

IN this chapter we propose to deal with the arrangement of passages for various combinations of woodwind and horns, but before doing this we will deal with the question of laying out full chords for the wind.

In order to obtain as uniform and homogeneous a texture as possible the principle known as 'dovetailing' is used. If, for instance, the chord [music] were laid out for oboes and clarinets thus [music] the resulting blend would be less satisfactory than this: [music] in which the reedy oboe and the smoother clarinet tone are inextricably intermingled. The same principle holds good for all pairs of wind instruments in combination unless, of course, the two bottom notes of the chord lie outside the downward compass of the upper pair of instruments.

This chord [music] for instance, could only be laid out in the manner indicated, but the blend would hardly be impaired at all owing to the thick reediness of the low clarinets.

The case of the flutes and oboes requires a little more judgement, for, if the chord were high-placed, dovetailing would result in the 1st oboe playing in its thinnest and least effective register, e.g. [music]

On the other hand, in a medium-placed chord, the 2nd flute might find itself too low to compete with the rest, owing to the comparative weakness of the flute in its lowest register, e.g. [music] The above chords would therefore be scored best in this way: [music]

The same remarks apply to the combination of flutes and clarinets.

34

Indiscriminate enthusiasm for dove-tailing may also sometimes lead to the 1st horn being placed too high. This, of course, results in his note 'sticking out' from the chord, especially if it is a quiet one.

Briefly then, the rule of dovetailing (like all other artistic laws) must not take precedence of common sense, but must be regarded as the normal procedure, and deviations from it as exceptions requiring justification.

In laying out a chord which covers a wide range the bottom two octaves or so should be less densely populated with notes than the higher altitudes. Just as the members of the harmonic series come at closer and closer intervals as the series ascends, so will the notes of a well-sounding chord be arranged with the notes which make up the top half closer together than those of the bottom half, and a clear octave should be left at the extreme bottom of the chord.

We will now lay out various chords for double woodwind and two horns. To save space these are condensed on two staves. The beginner would be well advised to copy them out in open score with the necessary transpositions.

Ex. IX

Chord of B♭ (soft)

Note the dovetailing of all the pairs of instruments except flutes and oboes, and the deep solid octave-combination of 2nd horn and 2nd bassoon at the bottom of the chord.

Ex. X

Chord of A♭ (loud)

Here the clarinets are placed above the oboes and would thus give a clear brilliant 'tang' to the chord. The oboe tends to lose power and body in its upper register, but with the clarinet the opposite is the case. The horns play the root of the chord and are placed considerably higher than

35

they are in Ex. IX for greater resonance and strength. It will be noted that they are marked *mf* or *f* against the *f* or *ff* of the rest of the ensemble to guard against their upsetting the balance by too powerful and brassy a tone.

Ex. XI

Chord of G, 1st inversion

Here we have a wide-spread quiet ⁶₃ chord. Its effect should be very full and rich. The bass of a 1st inversion should not be doubled in any of the upper parts if a clear, clean sonority is aimed at. The ordinary rules regarding doubling the bass in four-part harmony should be followed unless, of course, a passage is written in more than four 'real' parts. The bass may, however, always be doubled at the octave *below* if desired.

Ex. XII

Dom. 7th of G, 1st inversion
with resolution on to tonic chord

All the parts here resolve on to their appointed notes. It should be obvious that a dissonance sounded by one instrument must be resolved by that instrument (unless there is a complete break-off and a rest or pause separating the discord from what follows), but it is the writer's experience that beginners do not always realize the musical necessity for this.

This principle applies in full force in dealing with the harmonic idioms of the present day, in which discords are approached and quitted with the utmost freedom, and there is often little or no feeling of resolution at all, for there must always be 'part-writing' and the notes must 'go somewhere' and not be left in the air, so to speak, even if the progressions are not in accord with nineteenth-century harmonic notions.

Most octave-combinations of wind instruments are effective and each has its distinct character. The flute adds brightness to oboe, clarinet, bassoon, and horn when it doubles them at the octave. It also forms a

36

fascinating double-octave combination with the clarinet and also (as above mentioned) with the bassoon. The octave of oboe and clarinet is not very satisfactory, but those of oboe and bassoon or oboe and horn are of excellent effect, particularly the latter. Clarinet and bassoon in octaves or at two octaves distance sound very well indeed; clarinet and horn, too, make an excellent blend. A good effect, especially if a mildly bizarre or impertinent characterization is required, is that obtained from two clarinets at two octaves distance, one in its upper register and the other in its chalumeau, and if an oboe is added in the middle octave the reediness is much enhanced and the penetrating power of the combination greatly increased.

On the whole, perhaps, octave-combinations are of better effect and are more powerful and telling than actual unisons between instruments of diverse timbres. These, however, are freely used either to obtain further variation of colour or to strengthen a melodic line which would be too weak on a single wind instrument.*

Good unisons are those formed by flute and oboe (in the low and middle registers of the flute), flute and clarinet (in all available registers), flute and bassoon (flute of course in its low register, and bassoon near the top of its compass), flute and horn (flute low again here, naturally).

The oboe in unison with the clarinet imparts to the latter a cutting edge, and the resulting sound is quite agreeable in small quantities. Lowish oboe and high bassoon sound of course very reedy and rather exotic. The oboe and horn are not satisfactory in unison—they blend insufficiently. The clarinet added to the upper notes of the bassoon improves the tone of the latter, and low clarinet and medium bassoon notes are rich and powerful in combination. The clarinet and horn blend quite well in unison also.

The bassoon, in addition to the unison-combinations in which it figures above, blends very well with the horn without removing from the latter its distinguished quality of tone.

The power of any of the above may be doubled by using two of each instrument, or if preponderance of one tone-colour were required, a pair of one sort of instrument would be combined with a single instrument of another sort (e.g. 2 clar.+1 ob.). Slight imperfections of intonation are less noticeable, by the way, between two pairs of instruments combined in unison than between two single instruments so combined.

* Unison doublings should be very sparingly employed in all but the *full* orchestra.

37

The use of a pair each of clarinets, bassoons, and horns in unison produces a rich powerful ensemble of great depth and beauty of tone. The unison of flutes, oboes, and clarinets is also of considerable power and uniformity of tone (the oboes perhaps slightly predominating).

When a pair of instruments of the same sort is to be used in unison. the passage is marked à 2. When the first of the pair is to be used alone the tails of the notes should all be turned upwards, and rests for the second player placed below. When the second player plays alone the process is reversed.

E.g. Horns in F

Where a single instrument has the principal melody or an important phrase the passage is marked SOLO (when more than one instrument is involved use the plural SOLI). At the cessation of the solo passage, if the instrument continues to play but only has a subordinate part, it is a good plan to place an asterisk at the point where the prominent passage ends. Since this practice is not yet by any means universal, and the player may not have come across it before, a note of explanation should be given at the beginning of the part, otherwise the asterisk will cause the player to look for a footnote at the bottom of the page. If a rest follows the solo passage the asterisk is unnecessary.

Try to arrange things in such a way that a player has a few bars' rest before his solo passage begins. This enables him to have a short 'breather' in preparation, and also draws the attention of the audience to him more surely when his solo arrives. (This is analogous to the short rests usually given to a fugal 'voice' before a 'middle entry' of the subject.)

It is exceptional to find passages of any great length scored only for wind instruments, but short passages which lend themselves readily and easily to such treatment are of excellent effect and provide good contrast. Since the blend of the wind-group is not so perfect as that of the strings, owing to the greater uniformity of tone of the latter, passages of which the texture can be resolved into its component patterns, each of which suits the individual character of some particular instrument or small group of instruments, 'come off' best on the wind. In short, those passages which rely for their effect on colour-contrasts rather than on colour-blending are most suitable for wind alone. A succession of full chords for wind and horns bears a rather oppressive resemblance to the sound of a harmonium if it continues for many bars without relief.

We will now give a few examples of short passages scored for woodwind and horns.

Grieg—Pianoforte Sonata

Ex. XIII

2 Fl.

2 Ob.

2 Clar. in Bb

2 Fag.

2 Hns.

39

This shows a little phrase handed from one instrument to another. Note, in the second bar, that it is the 2nd clarinet which completes the chord on the flutes because the 1st clarinet has a solo passage in the next bar. In the third and fourth bars the two flutes play in unison in order to balance with the oboes and clarinets. This, of course, would not be necessary if the flute part were not rather low and hence weak by comparison. In the seventh bar the bottom A♭ of the chord has, unfortunately, to be omitted, being too low for the bassoons. The chord would, however, probably 'sound lower than it is' owing to its deep and dense sonority, and the absence of the lower octave would thus hardly be felt. One very small point of procedure is worth noting: at a first glance at this example there appears to be a redundancy of the indication *pp*, but on closer examination it is seen that it has never been used unnecessarily, for where it appears on the same line of the score in two successive bars the first of the pair of instruments whose parts are written on that line enters alone, and the second joins him in the next bar. They thus each require the *pp*, as their parts are copied either on separate sheets or at any rate on separate lines on the same sheet. (Cf. p. 17, remarks on accidentals in string divisi.)

In the example opposite, an antiphonal effect is evidently required between bars 1 and 2 and bars 3 and 4. It is therefore necessary to find two contrasted groups of instruments. As scored here the woodwind and horns are pitted against each other, the character of the music, with its fanfare-like subject lending itself well to such treatment. The bassoons are required for both groups. In bar 4 the combination of 1st bassoon and horns would give the effect of a chord on three horns. (Remember that this would not hold good if the passage were *f* instead of *p*.)

The flutes could be omitted without loss of anything essential. They are added here to give brightness and to enhance the contrast with the horns. The downward arpeggio in the last two bars will obviously be given to the clarinet, for besides the fact that it fits that instrument like a glove, it does not lie within the range of any other wind instrument. The 1st clarinet is therefore held in reserve until the high F is reached four bars from the end of the extract, thus drawing the attention of the audience unconsciously to that note and preparing the way for its little solo passage. The 1st oboe plays the top line in the preceding four bars,

Ex. XIV

Schumann—Faschingsschwank aus Wien

and gives place to the 1st clarinet on reaching the aforesaid high F. Note the smooth movement of the horns in the chord-passage, and the introduction of the 2nd clarinet on the low E to complete the harmony at the sixth bar from the end. Owing to the crescendo, the 2nd clarinet, when once it has entered, cannot be dropped and is therefore carried on That is the reason for the presence of the low F on the 2nd clarinet in the final chord—a note which is not in the original piano score. (The 1st oboe can, of course, be dropped without impairing the sense of climax, as its place is actually taken by the 1st clarinet.)

Ex. XV   Tschaikovsky— Scherzo, Op. 21. No 6

Here the principal melodic line is divided between horn, oboe, and bassoon, and later between horn, oboe, and clarinet. The semiquaver decorations are given to the flutes except for one short passage which goes too low for the flute, and is taken by the clarinet. The 2nd flute relieves the 1st at one point by taking over the decorations. Such a long passage without any breathing spaces would be trying for a single player, who would have to fit in an intake of breath where the phrasing breaks. This would occupy a fraction of a second which would have to be made up by hurrying over the next group of semiquavers, and would sound breathless and hectic. Of course, if the 2nd flute (in an amateur orchestra) were unequal to the strain of facing the glare of even such ephemeral publicity, the arranger would be wiser to 'temper the wind' and let the 1st flute play the whole passage.

Note the *pp* of the horn against the *p* of clarinet and bassoons in the last two bars, where it is merely completing their harmony.

Thinness of texture has been guarded against by means of the bassoon parts in bar 2 and the bassoon parts in bars 6 and 7 (in which the implied bass is given on the 2nd, 3rd, and 4th quaver-beats of each bar).

Ex. XVI needs little comment. Note the lay-out of the alternating chords in the first four bars. The muted horn-notes are an unessential addition but would materially increase the bizarre effect of the passage as a whole. In the last four bars the melodic line is carried by the two clarinets in unison, and extra grace-notes which do not appear in the original are given to 2nd flute and 2nd oboe with the object of enhancing the suggestion of the chirping and clucking of chickens. In music of a

43

Ex. XVI

Moussorgsky — Ballet de Poussins dans leurs Coques
(Tableaux d'une exposition)

definitely pictorial kind such as this, every effort must be made in the direction of realism, provided that no violence is done to the musical outline of the original.

EXERCISES

The following are suggested as suitable exercises in scoring for woodwind and horns.

1. Beethoven, 'Tempo di Menuetto' from Sonata in G, Op. 49, No. 2.
2. Beethoven, 3rd movt. (omitting Trio), from Sonata in E flat, Op. 7.
3. Schumann, Romanze from Faschingsschwank aus Wien.
4. Chopin, Prelude in A major, No. 7 of Twenty-four Preludes.
5. Grieg, Elfentanz (in E minor), from Lyric Pieces.
6. Macdowell, 'From Uncle Remus', Woodland Sketches, Op. 51, No. 7.[1]
7. Debussy, 'The Little Shepherd', Children's Corner, No. 5.[2]
8. Eugène Goossens, 'The Hurdy-Gurdy Man', Kaleidoscope, Op. 18, No. 3.[3]
9. Eugène Goossens, 'Lament for a Departed Doll', ibid., No. 10.

[1] Elkin & Co., Ltd. [2] A Durand et Fils. [3] J. & W. Chester.

CHAPTER V

THE SMALL ORCHESTRA

(WOODWIND, HORNS, AND STRINGS)

W E will now consider the combination of strings, woodwind, and horns. The student will find an unlimited number of examples of effective writing for this combination in orchestral works of all schools from Haydn onwards. The symphonies of Haydn and Mozart of course provide the simplest (and hence some of the very best) models since, even when the score contains trumpets and drums, these are nearly always used simply for noise-making purposes, and the bulk of the work is allotted to strings, woodwind, and horns.

The strings, owing to their flexibility, expressiveness, and pre-eminently satisfying tone-colour, form the foundation of the orchestra and are frequently used alone. The wind group, as we have said, less frequently stands alone, and then only for a few bars at a time. Beginners, however, almost always try to secure contrast by alternating passages for strings and wind, and experience great difficulty in satisfactorily combining the two groups.

The following table, based on an analysis of ten movements taken quite at random from the works of Mozart, Beethoven, Mendelssohn, Berlioz, Wagner, and Tschaikovsky, may be of interest in this connexion:

Total no. of bars in the ten works	No. of bars in which strings play alone	No. of bars in which wind plays alone	Sum of longest passages in each work for strings	Sum of longest passages in each work for wind	No. of bars in which strings and wind play together
2,912	496 (17%)	136 (5%)	134 (5%)	57 (2%)	2,270 (78%)

Of course it would be the height of absurdity to lay down a rule that these proportions should even approximately be aimed at in every orchestral movement. It goes without saying that everything depends on the nature of the piece of music to be scored. Cases in which prolonged antiphonal use of wind and strings is suitable will, however, be rare, as

46

such treatment tends, naturally, to produce a sense of discontinuity. One cannot repeat too often that good scoring is the result of intelligent listening, and the student is strongly advised to cultivate his orchestral ear by following with the score. This, however, is of little use unless the score has been fully studied beforehand, and the passages of which the effect cannot be heard mentally marked for special attention at performance. Those who are pupils of the large schools of music will have the great advantage of hearing a good many standard works rehearsed many times by the students' orchestra, or perhaps even of playing in them. Others who have not this privilege would be well advised to listen carefully to good gramophone records with the score, and to go over many times passages which seem to them obscure or unfamiliar in sound at a first hearing. Those who cannot afford to go to many concerts or buy expensive records (and few music-students can!), or who live far from the centres of music-making, can hear much good orchestral music by wireless. Some musicians declare that 'all the instruments sound the same' on the wireless, but this is not the writer's experience, though he would be the first to admit that hearing the 'real thing' after a course of wireless listening is very much like seeing, say, the Botticelli Venus after making its acquaintance through the medium of a Medici print.

We will now score a few short extracts chosen to illustrate various points of treatment.

Ex. XVII

Beethoven — Sonata in E minor Op. 90

a) Allegro

b) Andantino

Mozart — Fantasia

In Ex. XVII, a) and b), the lay-out is so obvious that it is unnecessary to print them in score. They show two cases in which antiphonal treatment of strings and wind would be suitable. This is so because of the strongly marked contrast between the opening and responsive phrases in each passage. Our orchestration must therefore enhance these contrasts in the strongest possible way, namely by alternating the strings with a wind group.

Ex. XVIII   Beethoven— Sonata in D, Op. 10. No. 3, 2nd movement

This passage (Ex. XVIII) seems to demand a dark but sonorous tone-colour. The melody must stand out clearly from the accompanying chords and must be richly expressive and sustained. The word 'expressive' gives us our clue. We have said that the strings are the most expressive and flexible group in the orchestra. We will therefore allot the melody to the whole of the strings except double basses, and give the accompanying chords to a suitable wind group, doubling the bass with the double basses for greater depth and impressiveness. The 1st and 2nd violins will play the upper octave of the melody in unison on the G string, and the violas and 'cellos the lower octave. The violas, as we know, being on their C string will impart a dark and strongly characterized tone-colour to the 'cellos who will be playing in a very sweet and expressive though rather sombre part of their compass.

48

So much for the melodic line. We now turn our attention to the accompanying wind chords. It would of course be possible to give them to clarinets and bassoons (let us hope that no one would wish to use an oboe for the top note of the chords—it would be terribly nasal and obtrusive here, on its bottom notes), but the low-placed clarinets would sound rather too hollow and 'woody' for the rich effect we have in mind. What else can we use? Why, the horns! They will give us exactly the colour we want, especially if we dovetail them with the bassoons and thus make use of the deep low notes of the second horn. The dovetailing will also give us a perfectly homogeneous blend, for we know from our studies of wind alone how well horns and bassoons combine. (Think of the opening chords of the slow movement of Schubert's 'Unfinished', for instance.) We thus have an example of a string melody accompanied by wind. It is hardly necessary to say that this is only one way of scoring this passage. To some, for instance, the melody with its conjunct movement might suggest the beautifully expressive horn colour doubled at the lower octave by a bassoon. In this case the strings would no doubt be used for

49

the accompanying chords, forming as is their wont when required, a perfect background. This arrangement would lack the sonority of that which we have given, but the beauty of the horn in a melody which would suit it so well would be a point very much in its favour.

Neither arrangement is more 'right' than the other. The final choice lies solely with individual preference.

Ex. XIX

Debussy — Toccata, Bars 62–71

Ex. XIX, which is highly pianistic, demands great brilliance and strong rhythm together with a complete contrast in the last two bars of the extract. In our arrangement we have allotted the semiquavers to 1st and 2nd violins while the unison of two flutes and two oboes provides an 'imitation trumpet' effect above them. The martellato in the left-hand part of the original is provided by *pizzicato* violas and 'cellos in unison doubled by the clarinets and later by the horns. Note the way in which the pianistic idiom in bars 3 and 4 has been translated into its orchestral equivalent, and the use of the bassoons in bars 7 and 8 which prevents the otherwise somewhat tenuous texture from falling to pieces.

50

Here we have another extract from the same work. Our arrangement needs no explanation, but the simplification of the double-bass part

Ex. XX   Debussy — Toccata, Bars 162–168

(a very ordinary orchestral procedure), the use of the low notes of the clarinet, and the combination of reiterated notes on the violas with the same notes played legato by the bassoons should be noted.

Rhythm and 'snap' are the chief characteristics of Ex. XXI. We have decided to amplify the chords by reduplicating them in the higher octave in order to obtain greater clearness and bite. Clarinets and bassoons supply the melodic part of the texture, while the oboes are allotted the reiterated notes, and flutes, horns, and *pizzicati* strings give weight to the accented chords which occur at the end of each bar and the beginning of the next. The strings (with the flutes added at the octave above) give the right feeling of impetuousness to the arpeggio in the final bar of the extract, the held octave F of the horns preventing any suspicion of thinness here. The double basses have but one note to play, but we venture to think it an effective one; the dry thud of this high *pizzicato* note would appear to liberate the rush of the strings which immediately follows it. Possibly a little touch like this has more meaning for us, belonging as we do to a mechanical age, than it would have had for our

52

Ex. XXI

VAR. VII — Brahms — Variations and Fugue on a theme of Handel

grandfathers, who were unaccustomed to the click of an electric switch and its attendant results!

The possibilities of the small orchestra are so immense—almost infinite—that it would be profitless to add further examples, especially as there is an unlimited number of models to be found among the works of the great masters of orchestration from Haydn to the present day. We would earnestly advise the student to 'get the miniature score habit' (to use the jargon of the advertisement writers). All sorts of odd moments occur during the day, in which a page or two of a score can be read and hints stored away for future use. Apart from all else the concentration required to hear mentally an orchestral passage while seated in an omnibus or train or standing in the Underground cannot fail to be beneficial.

Before concluding this chapter a few remarks on the subject of doubling strings by wind may be useful. We will take each member of the string group in turn. It must be remembered that these remarks apply only in the case of the *small* orchestra, in which string and wind doubling is rarely necessary for the sake of balance. In the full orchestra such doubling is frequently a necessity owing to the tremendous swamping-power of the heavy brass.

1. *The Violins.*

Not much is to be gained by *unison* doubling except in passages where the G string is in use. Clarinets or horns or both together may be used if a very rich sound is required. The unison of violins and oboe is unsatisfactory unless there is a large mass of violins. Avoid it, therefore, in the small orchestra. The oboe tends to impoverish the tone of the violins and to make it sound thin and pinched. The bottom five notes or so of the violins can be enriched by adding a bassoon or two in unison. Above that limit the bassoons begin to sound rather thin and thus fail to fulfil the desired object.

The violins may be doubled at the *higher* octave by a flute or two with very good effect. Not so by the oboe or clarinet. At the *lower* octave the bassoon is by far the best, though the bottom notes of the clarinet might be used (pitch permitting) if a dark, cloudy, and rather menacing atmosphere were desired. The violins and horn do not form a very good octave combination as they fail to blend. If both are muted, however, a strange and attractive tone-colour is produced in the pianissimo, but this is only suitable, naturally, for very special effects. The sound is better, perhaps, when the horn is an octave lower than the violins than vice versa.

2. *The Violas.*

The violas blend very well with most of the wind instruments. Indeed, in the string orchestra, they often give the illusion that bassoons or horns are playing. Next to these instruments the violas blend best in

55

unison with the clarinet, especially in the chalumeau register of the latter. If it is desired to emphasize the penetrating, rather reedy quality of the higher viola notes an oboe or two added in unison will do this, while two flutes in unison with the violas will produce the opposite effect by rounding off the tone. The unison of flutes, oboes, clarinets, and violas is powerful and striking, but is more likely to be found appropriate in the full orchestra than in the small orchestra. With regard to octave combinations, flute or oboe double the violas well at the higher octave, and bassoon at the lower octave, but opportunities of using these are rather rare, as the violas are of course chiefly used to supply inner parts either in the nature of harmonic filling up, or countermelodies in which octave doubling would upset the harmonic scheme.

3. The 'Cellos.

The unison of 'cellos and bassoons is of constant occurrence when a smooth sonorous bass is required. For slow-moving expressive passages in the tenor register a horn or two added to the 'cellos produces a very beautiful rich tone-quality in p and mf. The same combination is very powerful and forceful in f and ff. The addition of oboes to a high melodic 'cello passage gives it great poignancy, and at the same time counteracts the tendency towards thinness of tone which is apt to be somewhat distressing unless the 'cellos are both first-rate and numerous. The 'cello-oboe octave combination (the oboes, of course, above) is very good in a delicate p or pp melody. The octave-blend is less good between 'cellos and flute or clarinet.

4. The Double Basses.

The double bass-bassoon unison supplies a good bass in cases where the 'cellos are independently occupied. Where a light but well-defined bass is required, the double basses *pizzicati* might double the bassoons playing *legato*.

The octave combinations are practically confined, in the small orchestra, to

1. Double bass and bassoon.
2. Double bass and horn (for deep pedal notes only).

EXERCISES

The following are suggested as suitable exercises in scoring for woodwind, horns, and strings:

1. Beethoven, Sonata in A, Op. 2, No. 2. Largo appassionato and Scherzo.
2. Beethoven, Sonata in F, Op. 10, No. 2. Finale (Presto).
3. Schumann, 'Faschingsschwank aus Wien', Op. 26. Finale.[1]
4. Schumann, 'Kinderscenen', Op. 15.
5. Tschaikovsky, Humoreske in G, Op. 10, No. 2.
6. Grieg, 'Nordische Tänze und Volksweisen', Op. 17, Nos. 7, 18, 20, 24.
7. Grieg, 'Norwegische Volksweisen', Op. 66, Nos. 1, 2, 16.
8. Debussy, 'Suite bergamasque'. Prelude and Minuet.[2]
9. Debussy, 'Arabesque', No. 2 in G.

[1] Score the opening thus :

[2] The glissando in the third bar from the end of the Minuet will have to be shortened so as to end an octave lower than in the original. It will of course be given to the flute.

For further exercises see Appendix.

CHAPTER VI

THE BRASS

IN this chapter we propose to deal with the trumpets, trombones, and tuba.

The normal specification for the brass department of the full orchestra is as follows:

    4 horns
    2 trumpets
    3 trombones (2 tenor and 1 bass)
    1 tuba

The student will no doubt come across modern scores in which these numbers are exceeded (e.g. among the works of Wagner, Strauss, Scriabin, Stravinsky, Holst, &c.), but the above specification is, as we have said, the normal one and it is inadvisable for economic reasons to expand it unless, of course, extra instruments are absolutely indispensable for the full expression of the composer's ideas.

It is unnecessary to add much to what has been said already about the horn, except to point out that owing to its conical mouthpiece and bore it is unable to produce such a loud and brilliant tone as the trumpets and trombones, which are played with a cup-shaped mouthpiece and have a cylindrical bore over the greater part of their length.

In order to obtain perfect balance, therefore, in combining horns with trumpets or trombones, it is necessary to remember that 2 horns=1 trumpet or 1 trombone in dynamic ranges above and including *mezzo-forte*. Below *mezzo-forte*, 1 horn is sufficient to compete successfully with 1 trumpet or 1 trombone. When 4 horns are used, the 1st and 2nd

must be dovetailed with the 3rd and 4th, thus:

The 1st and 3rd specialize in the higher notes, the 2nd and 4th in the lower.

1. *The Trumpet.*

The trumpet, like the horn, was originally a 'natural' instrument which

was only able to obtain the notes of the harmonic series from its fundamental note, whatever that happened to be. Hence trumpets crooked in
all keys are to be found in scores of the classical period. Later, when the
valve-trumpet had permanently ousted the natural trumpet from the
orchestra, trumpets in F, A, B♭, and C were those in most general use.
Those in F and A have now dropped out of use (perhaps one of the most
recent scores in which parts are written for trumpets in F is Vaughan
Williams's 'London' Symphony, which was composed shortly before the
war of 1914–18) and though many modern composers write for the C
trumpet the B♭ instrument is used in this country almost exclusively.
The C trumpet, though brilliant and flexible, lacks nobility of tone and
its use is therefore not to be encouraged. The A trumpet may be used
for extreme sharp keys but in general it is better to keep to the B♭
instrument.

Many trumpet players possess a small trumpet in D which they use
for trumpet parts of the Bach-Handel period. In special circumstances
where a very high trumpet part is wanted this can be used.

The compass of the trumpet is

These are the *written* notes. On the B♭ trumpet the sounds are a tone
lower, on the A a minor third lower as in the case of clarinets. On the
D instrument the sounds are a tone higher.

The notes from   should be used with care and reserved

for 'high lights'. They are brilliantly effective if sparingly used. Up to
high G any note in the instrument's compass can be produced from *ppp*
to *fff* with ease and certainty.

The trumpet is capable of considerable agility, but it is as well not to
write rapid passages for it of any great length. By means of technical
methods known as single, double, and triple tonguing extremely rapid

but clear *staccato* production is obtainable, which is most sure and effective when used for the rapid reiteration of a single note, e.g.:

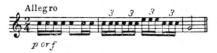

Passages requiring rapid tonguing should not, however, be continued long without brief rests or points of repose. Remember that the player is only a human being after all, and needs breathing spaces.

There is always danger in giving a melody of a sustained or lyrical nature to the trumpet, in fact this practice should be rigidly avoided. The similarity of tone between trumpet and cornet makes it impossible to listen to a lyrical tune on the trumpet without being immediately reminded of 'The Lost Chord' or of a Gilbert and Sullivan selection played by a brass or military band 'with the expression put in'! On the other hand, direct, rhythmical, rather square-cut tunes, or extremely slow-moving and dignified ones without a trace of sentimentality about them, can be allotted to the trumpet without qualms as to possible vulgarity of effect.

The mute when applied to the trumpet produces, when the instrument is blown softly, a far-away effect which, though not nearly so poetical as the sound of a soft muted horn, is nevertheless beautiful and intriguing. When blown loudly and forcibly a bizarre, grotesque sound results which has lately been exploited *ad nauseam*. Trumpet players in dance bands possess many different sorts of mutes with a corresponding number of resultant timbres. These might be studied by 'serious composers', as they would probably yield new and interesting effects if skilfully combined with other instruments such as low flutes, clarinets, &c.

2. *The Tenor Trombone* (in B♭, non-transposing).

In this instrument differences of pitch are obtained, not by the use of valves, as in the horn and trumpet, but by varying the length of the vibrating column of air by means of a movable slide, the position of which is altered at will by the player.

There are seven 'positions' each of which gives the player a different series of notes (consisting of course of the now familiar members of the harmonic series).

The instrument, when the slide is unextended stands in B♭, its lowest

note being

(This is the first harmonic from)

In this position (the 'first position') the following notes can be obtained:

In the second position the notes obtainable stand a semitone below the above, and so on through all the positions until the seventh position is reached, which stands a diminished 5th below the first:

seventh position

The compass of the tenor trombone, then, is (with four more possible semitones above).

The fundamental notes in all seven positions are also obtainable:

 &c., down to E.

These are called 'pedal notes'. Their use is not to be recommended as they are poor in quality. Forsyth, in his *Orchestration*, quotes a passage from Berlioz's 'Requiem' in which chords on three flutes are combined with pedal notes four octaves below on eight tenor trombones in unison, and remarks that 'it probably sounds very nasty'. The present writer has heard the passage. It does!

The tenor clef is the normal one used for tenor trombones, the bass clef being used for the bottom fifth or so of their compass.

3. *The Bass Trombone* (in **G**, non-transposing).

The compass of this instrument is

Its part is written exclusively in the bass clef. Pedal notes are obtainable on the bass trombone.

Most bass trombones are now fitted with an extension whereby all the semitones between the Bottom C♯ and the first pedal note G can be obtained. Its tone is more weighty than that of the tenor trombone, and its lowest notes are of better quality owing to the relative wideness of its bore.

It should not be employed for too long at a stretch without adequate breathing spaces, as it makes great demands on the physical endurance of the player.

4. *The Trombones in combination.*

Though the trombones are capable, in a limited degree, of a certain amount of rapidity of execution, opportunities for the exploitation of their powers in this direction are rare in the orchestra. They are best thought of as a three-part harmonic combination, chords on three trombones being extremely impressive in effect at all dynamic levels. In soft chords it is best to place them fairly low and in extended spacing, e.g.:

Ex. XXII

When an effect of blazing brilliance is aimed at, they should be placed higher, either in extended or close position, e.g.:

Ex. XXIII

It is useless to write long, sustained chords for the trombones at dynamic strengths above *mf*. They require too much breath, and result in a *fp* or at any rate a *f* > effect. Detached *f* or *ff* chords are extremely effective and have a tremendous rhythmical—almost percussive—effect, e.g.:

Ex. XXIV

It is a mistake to imagine that the sole function of the trombones is to make an overwhelming noise. This is, admittedly, one of their important duties, but their capacity for *pianissimo* delivery is very great, and the essential nobility of the trombone tone remains unchanged at all dynamic degrees. Soft chords spaced as in **Ex. XXII** above have a rich glow, and form a fine background for string, woodwind, or horn solos. Elgar has used trombone chords with masterly effect in the slow movement of his violin concerto to accompany the solo instrument for a few bars. These passages are well worth study ((i) 3rd bar after **No. 49** et seq.; (ii) 6th bar after No. 59 et seq.). It will be noticed that the 1st and 2nd trombones cross frequently in order to avoid wide changes of position as much as possible and consequently to obtain the maximum degree of smoothness. (Miniature score published by Novello's.)

When muted and blown hard the trombone produces an extravagantly nasal and metallic sound which, like that of the muted trumpet, has been robbed of much of its once undoubtedly humorous and grotesque significance by its over-exploitation in dance music.[1] The same may be said of the glissando, produced by rapidly drawing in or pushing out the slide.

The use of very quiet sustained chords on muted trombones has not yet, however, been done to death and is recommended as a luxury in which the orchestrator might very occasionally indulge.

The author craves to be forgiven for a very brief self-quotation in illustration of this from a work of his own:

Ex. XXV

The low flute-notes here stand out clearly against the almost inaudible muted trombone chord. A somewhat similar effect is to be found near the end of the slow movement of Vaughan Williams' Symphony in F minor.

5. *The Tuba* (in F, non-transposing).

This fine instrument, the deepest of the brass instruments of the orchestra, is usually associated with the trombones, though it is unlike them in every way. Like the horn and trumpet it is furnished with valves, but

[1] The effect of different kinds of mutes as in the case of the trumpet might, however, be profitably studied with a view to new and subtle tone-colours.

has four of these instead of three in order to give a complete chromatic scale from its fundamental note. Its compass is a large one,

The top octave is not, however, much used as a general rule except for very special solo effects where a relentless and rather brutal characterization is being aimed at. A few notes below the lowest note given above can be 'faked', but are not of very good quality. Their use (down to, say, D) is recommended only to complete the contour of a phrase which would otherwise lose its shape.

The obtrusive tone of the tuba makes it extremely useful in bringing important bass passages into prominence. It should be used somewhat sparingly, however, as it has a tendency, except in very full tuttis, to overload the bottom octaves of the orchestra.

Its everyday function is to provide a strong, firm bass to the trumpet-trombone group. In soft brass passages it provides a perfectly satisfactory bass by itself, but in loud ones the difference in quality between its 'blunt' tones and the 'sharp' utterance of the trumpets and trombones makes itself felt. It is therefore advisable to give the bass to the bass trombone and to double this at the octave below with the tuba.[1]

The tuba, when blown softly, combines well with the horns, and might be looked upon as a possible deep '5th horn'. It must be emphasized, however, that this amalgamation is only possible in the *p* and *pp*. The harder they are blown the more will the horns and tuba part company, until in the *ff* there is an almost complete lack of blend. These remarks apply only to cases in which horns and tuba are used alone, or almost alone. (Needless to say, *ff* horns and tuba can be used together when many other instruments are simultaneously at work and there is much 'doubling' going on.)

When using the tuba as an independent bass to the trombones in held chords the most satisfactory result is obtained if the tuba is placed rather low, even if this results in a big gap between it and the bass trombone. The writer ventures to think, for instance, that the final chord of the

[1] Sibelius' tuba parts should be studied. They show true awareness of the nature of the instrument.

1st movement of Tschaikovsky's 'Pathetic Symphony' would be more
satisfactory if arranged

If the above chord were required *f* or *ff* a good arrangement would be to
replace the 1st trombone by a trumpet, and to lay out the chord thus:

The chord is then complete on the sharp-toned instruments, the tuba
doubling the bass trombone at the octave below.

Other possibilities would be:

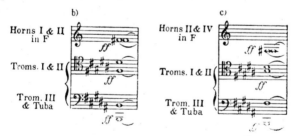

Arrangements (*b*) and (*c*) show the unison of two horns used to balance
with the trombones. (*c*) shows the 2nd and 4th horns (used here because
they are more accustomed to low notes than the 1st and 3rd) placed
below the trombones and an octave above the tuba. This gives a fine
solid bass to the chord which amalgamates excellently with the trombones
and is as good in *pp* as in *ff*.

The tuba, considering its size and depth, is surprisingly flexible and is capable also of a very light staccato. A good player has remarkable control over the instrument, and, though care needs to be exercised in its use owing to its obtrusive tone-quality, when not combined with other members of the 'heavy brass' family, composers (with some notable exceptions) are apt to be rather unenterprising in their handling of the instrument. Until some experience has been gained, however, the beginner would be well advised to use his tuba simply as a 'double bass' to the brass group, and to keep his tuba parts low. The bottom octave and a half of its compass is the best part of its range for everyday use.

For the sake of completeness it may be added that the tenor tuba (euphonium) is sometimes to be met with in modern scores in addition to the ordinary bass tuba (e.g., Strauss's 'Heldenleben' and 'Don Quixote', Holst's 'Planets').

The special quartet of small tubas used by Wagner in the 'Ring' need not detain us here. Information on this point is given in the article 'Tuba' in Grove's *Dictionary* and in Cecil Forsyth's admirable and encyclopaedic work *Orchestration* (Macmillan & Co. Ltd.).

This completes our brief description of the orchestral brass. We ought perhaps, however, to add a remark or two about the cornet, as the student may come across scores into which that instrument has found its way (e.g. Bizet's 'Carmen', Stravinsky's 'Petrouchka', Vaughan Williams' 'London' Symphony, Elgar's 'Cockaigne' Overture).

The cornet is in B♭ or A, transposes like the B♭ or A clarinet, and has the same compass as the trumpet in B♭ or A. It is operated in the same way as the trumpet, i.e. by means of three valves, and differs only from it in tone-quality (owing to its wider bore and larger mouthpiece), which is on the whole rounder and less brassy than that of the trumpet. Its articulation is easier and hence its flexibility is greater than that of the trumpet, but its proper place is the brass or military band and it has not succeeded in establishing itself permanently in the orchestra. Its use is therefore not to be recommended.

EXERCISES

Score the following pieces for the instruments indicated:

1. Grieg, 'National Song', *Lyric Pieces*, vol. i (Op. 12), No. 8; for 2 trumpets, 3 trombones, and tuba.

2. Grieg, 'Sailor's Song', *Lyric Pieces*, vol. ix (Op. 68), No. 1 ; for 4 horns, 2 trumpets, 3 trombones, and tuba.

3. Schumann, 'An important event', 'Kinderscenen' (Op. 15), No. 6; for 4 horns, 2 trumpets, 3 trombones, and tuba.

4. Moussorgsky, 'Promenade', Introduction to 'Pictures from an Exhibition'; for 4 horns, 2 trumpets, 3 trombones, and tuba.

CHAPTER VII

THE PERCUSSION

WE now come to a consideration of the percussion group (commonly known as 'the kitchen'), chief among which stand the *Timpani* (or kettledrums).

These consist of two or three drums in which the degree of tightness of the stretched vibrating skin (known as the 'head') can be adjusted to give notes of definite pitch.

Formerly, two drums only were used, tuned to the tonic and dominant of the piece to be played, but nowadays three are found in all well-equipped large orchestras and the tuning is determined by the orchestrator's choice.

When two drums are used, the upper drum can be tuned to any note

contained in the following interval:
(with possible F♯ and G above).

And the lower one: (with possible E♮ and E♭ below).

The third drum lies between these:

The notes to which the drums are to be tuned is stated at the beginning of the piece in score and part, e.g.:

Timpani in F, C, D   ( )

The actual pitch should be written in, as shown, when there would otherwise be ambiguity (as there would be in this case, as to which F is required, high or low).

The tuning of the drums is sometimes altered during a movement. It is advisable, however, not to alter the tuning of any one drum by more than a tone (since small alterations of tuning can be effected by 'feel' to a great extent), and a dozen or more bars of moderate time ought to be allowed for accurate adjustment of the tuning-screws.

The kettledrums are struck with felt-headed flexible sticks. The roll is indicated by the sign tr〜〜 over the note. When a roll is continued for several bars the note must be tied over to avoid a fresh attack on the succeeding first beats.

In addition to the roll, the kettledrums are effective in single strokes and in the execution of simple or complex rhythmical figures. Although they are employed to a much greater extent than the rest of the percussion, it must be realized that their effectiveness largely depends on a sparing use of them. Do not, however, regard the kettledrums as mere noise-makers. Strokes or rolls on the drums *pp* are a commonplace of orchestral writing. Be very sparing in the use of drums in passages where they are unable to supply a note of the harmony. It is better to leave them out altogether in most cases of this sort, however much you long to use them. Nothing obscures the outlines of an orchestral passage more than a drum roll on an unrelated note. Detached strokes can sometimes be used on dissonant notes, however, without damage.

The student who wishes to go farther into the matter of kettledrum technique is recommended to study *The Kettledrums*: Kirby (Oxford University Press), a very able and exhaustive treatise.

The Bass Drum.

This instrument must be familiar to every one who has ever heard a military band. Its part is usually written in the bass clef on the note C

It is struck with a rigid stick with a large head of felt. Single strokes at regular intervals on the bass drum *p* or *pp* are most impressive—almost awe-inspiring—and when *f* or *ff* impart tremendous force to the tutti. Owing to the depth and reverberation of the sound of the bass drum, rhythmical figures, unless very slow, do not come out clearly, but the roll is quite often used and is especially effective *pp*, when it imparts to the ensemble a 'shuddering' effect akin to that produced by a 32- or 64-foot organ-pipe. (Notation of roll same as for timpani.)

The Cymbals.

These are the familiar plates of metal which, when clashed together, produce the most shattering effect of which any orchestral instrument is capable. They are sometimes operated by the bass-drum player, one cymbal being strapped to the drum, the other held in the player's left hand, while he beats the drum with a drum-stick held in his right hand. The tone of the cymbals played thus is much inferior to that produced when a cymbal can be held in each hand so that both are free to vibrate equally when clashed together. Economic reasons, however, must be blamed for the prevalence of the former practice. It is best, therefore, to write bass drum and cymbals on the same staff so that one performer

can operate both if necessary, e.g.:

The direction 'laissez vibrer' is given here to indicate that the cymbals are to be allowed to vibrate freely—to ring on until their vibration dies away naturally. If the opposite effect is desired a note of short value is

written and the word 'sec' added, thus:

The cymbals are then 'damped' immediately after striking by drawing them sharply back against the player's body.

Special effects can be obtained by strokes or rolls on a suspended cymbal, executed with timpani or side-drum sticks. A single stroke on a cymbal with a timpani stick produces a 'splash' of sound, and a *crescendo* roll adds great excitement if added to a general orchestral *crescendo* three or four bars before its climax.

The notation of the roll is similar to that for the timpani roll. Side-drum sticks being made of hard unyielding wood without a soft head produce, of course, a much harder and more metallic sound than do the soft-headed timpani sticks. The kind of stick to be used must be stated.

Side-drum.

This, like the bass drum, has two 'heads', or vibrating surfaces, the upper head only being played on. The lower head has a few catgut strings stretched fairly tightly across it which give the 'rattle', which is the strongest characteristic of the sound of this drum. When these snares are loosened the tone becomes hollow and resonant. The drum is then said to be 'muffled'.

Owing to the tightness of the head, which causes the hard wooden sticks to rebound automatically, a very close roll is obtainable at all dynamic ranges. The dry crisp tone of the side-drum makes it an ideal instrument for emphasizing and giving clearness to rhythmical patterns of almost any speed and intricacy.

Very characteristic of the side-drum are the strokes known as the 'flam' and the 'drag'.

The drag, though usually appearing as above, may contain more than two preliminary grace-notes (which really amount to an infinitesimally short roll). These strokes are very much more effective than single strokes. A very loud explosive sound can be obtained, however, by striking the centre of the head hard with a kettledrum stick.

Side-drum parts are usually written in the treble clef on the note C, as above, but it must be clearly understood that *the side-drum never gives a note of definite pitch.* The roll, like that of the kettledrums, is indicated by the sign tr〰. A short *crescendo* roll (about two bars of moderate time) lends tremendous excitement to a big climax, and effects like this are extremely dramatic:

It is advisable in the interests of rhythmical 'tidiness' to end a roll of any kind (*pp*, *ff*, *cresc.*, or *dim.*) on a definite beat, and not to 'leave it in the air', e.g.:

The Triangle.

This is a metal bar bent into the shape of a triangle and struck with a metal beater. It gives a clear metallic ring. Single strokes are often used to mark the principal accents in the lighter forms of music. The roll, produced by ringing two adjacent sides of the triangle, when *ff*, is capable of coming through the *ff* of the full orchestra. Its part is generally written in the treble clef on B or G to distinguish it from the side-drum. It is of indefinite pitch.

The Tambourine.

This consists of a round wooden hoop across which a parchment head is stretched and to which loosely fitting metal plates, like tiny cymbals, are attached. These jingle at the slightest touch on the head. The instrument is held in the player's right hand, and struck with his left. The roll is produced by shaking the tambourine rapidly, or, more satisfactorily, by running the thumb (slightly moistened) of the left hand round the outside edge of the head. The latter method needs practice and knack, but gives a much closer roll than the former.

The use of the tambourine should be confined to dance music or to music of a dance-like character.

Its part is often written in the treble clef on G (2nd line) but it is quite immaterial which clef or note is used, provided that a note different from those used for the side-drum and triangle (if these appear in the same score) is chosen.

The instruments described above comprise all the percussion instruments in common use. Such things as the tenor drum, tubular bells, cow bells, jingles, castanets (useful for Spanish rhapsodies), gong (sinister, solemn, Chinese), tabor (Old English), &c., &c., need not be spoken of in detail. Their function is to supply realism or local colour, and for these purposes their use is perfectly legitimate.

The treatment of percussion in general.

Rimsky-Korsakoff has said with truth that love of percussion is the besetting sin of the budding orchestrator. One does not wish to appear in the role of kill-joy or pedant, but it really is true that these things lose their value enormously when they are used too much. We are not speaking here so much of the kettledrums, which are on a higher artistic plane than the rest of the 'kitchen', but with regard to the percussion instruments of indefinite pitch, one should be extremely sparing in their use. The admirably ingenious and astute orchestrators of jazz music have soon learned this. The prominence of the percussion which, in the early days of jazz, was responsible for such expressions as 'Tin-pan Alley' produced an effect of wearisome monotony which, if continued for long after the first flush of novelty had worn off, would have become unbearable. The discreet undertone of percussion as used in the best dance bands at the present day provides the necessary rhythmic basis and no more.

The best way of avoiding temptation is to make a habit, unless writing for an abnormally large orchestra, of employing only two percussion players, one for the kettledrums exclusively, and the other for the rest of the percussion. This practice has the merit of cutting down expense as well as of checking one's primitive barbaric instincts. In this case it will be as well not to use the bass drum and cymbals simultaneously (they do not really go particularly well together), so that the cymbals can be played in the proper way, one held in each hand.

A few bars rest are all that are required to change from one instrument to another so that plenty of variety of colour can be obtained in a short space if required. In this connexion it is worth remembering that it takes a little longer to change where cymbals are concerned (owing to the way in which they are held) but from bass drum to side-drum, triangle, or tambourine, or from any of these to any other is a matter of seconds. We here append a line or two of an imaginary one-man percussion part, in order to familiarize the student with the notation, the indications of changes of instrument, and the recognized abbreviations of their names:

Ex. XXVI

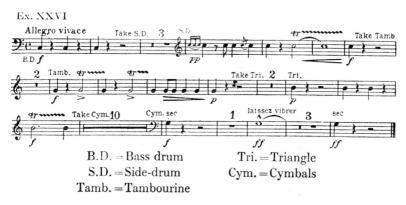

B.D. = Bass drum
S.D. = Side-drum
Tamb. = Tambourine
Tri. = Triangle
Cym. = Cymbals

CHAPTER VIII

THE HARP, GLOCKENSPIEL, XYLOPHONE, AND CELESTA

The Harp.

MUSIC for the harp is written on two staves exactly as is that for the pianoforte. The instrument is tuned to the diatonic scale of

C♭, its compass being:

Top G♮ and G♯ are also available by means of the pedal mechanism about to be explained.

The harp is provided with seven pedals, each one of which affects, when depressed, one of the notes of the scale in each octave of the instrument. When pressed down half-way, at which point it can be caught in a notch, the note is raised a semitone; when pressed down farther to the second notch the note is raised another semitone. We thus see the reason for the choice of C♭ for its normal key, since every note in the scale of C♭ can be raised one or two semitones *without changing its name.* Each string, then, is associated in the player's mind with a definite note, which is played on the same string whether it is flat, sharp, or natural, the pedals being alone responsible for the chromatic alterations. The harp can thus be 'set' in any desired key. It is not, however, confined to that key, for the pedals can be altered rapidly, and chromatic alterations of a note or two in successive chords in slow time are possible. It is evident, however, that much care has to be taken not to have too quick alterations nor too many at a time. With a little ingenuity, passages which at first sight would appear to require much use of the pedals can often be made playable with very little chromatic alteration, or perhaps none at all, by using enharmonic equivalents of certain notes. This usually makes the chords *look* rather queer on paper, but this does not worry the harpist, who, as we have said, connects each note, whatever

74

its chromatic inflexion, with a particular string. An example or two will make this clear.

This would necessitate a constant and irritating alteration of E♮ to E♭ and back again.

By substituting D♯ for E♭, no change of pedal is needed:

The following succession of chords

necessitates a change from A to A♯ and no more if the harp is set to these notes: D, E♯, F♯, G♯, A, B♯, C♯, for they are then written thus:

Double sharps and double flats should always be replaced by their enharmonic equivalents in harp writing. Passages based on chords or arpeggios are equally effective on the harp. It is rarely used as a solo instrument (at any rate melodically) but is inimitable as a means of enriching an orchestral background. It forms an excellent accompaniment to string or woodwind solos, either by itself or in conjunction with quiet, held string or wind chords. Harp chords add great resonance to *pizzicato* strings.

In writing chords for the harp, the two hands should be kept close together, and the chords well filled in. Chords which would sound thick and dull on the pianoforte do not sound so on the harp. In arpeggios

75

divided between the hands the same rule holds good. Tenths can be stretched easily on the harp. Do not, however, write chords of more than four notes in each hand. The little finger is not used in harp-playing.

Harp glissandos are frequently used. They are executed by drawing a finger rapidly up or down the strings. By means of what one might call 'fancy tunings', in which certain notes are reduplicated enharmonically (e.g. E♮ on the E string, and F♭ on the F), glissandos other than ordinary major and minor scales can be obtained, *provided every string is accounted for.* For instance a glissando based on the chord of the 'added 6th' might be desired, such as the following:

This means that only four notes in each octave are wanted instead of the normal seven, yet all seven must be accounted for to make the glissando possible. The following tuning gives us what we want.

$$E♮, F♭ \quad G♯, A♭ \quad B♮ C♭ \quad D♭$$
$$\underbrace{}_{E} \quad \underbrace{}_{G♯} \quad \underbrace{}_{B} \quad \underbrace{}_{C♯}$$

The glissando is so rapid that the repetitions of certain notes in it are not heard.

The student will find that *all* 'added 6ths' cannot be arranged as above. He might try one, for instance, starting on F♮ or C♮ instead of E, and see what happens. He will find, however, that all chords of the diminished 7th and some of the 'leading 7th' and dominant 7th can be obtained, also the two whole-tone scales, &c.

When writing glissandos it is not necessary to give more than the first and last notes of the glissando, if the notes to which the harp is to be set are given. A straight line joining the two notes with the word 'gliss.' added is all that is required.

Here are a few bars of an imaginary harp part, to make the method of notation clear:

The harp is here set to the dominant 7th in the key of E. Six bars rest provide time and to spare for setting the pedals. The glissando begins on the second beat, reaches its upward limit on the third, returns to its starting-point on the fourth, and ends on the first beat of the next bar.

Glissandos should be made as long as possible, as they are ineffective unless very rapidly executed. The passage above is marked *molto moderato*. At quicker speeds the glissandos would have to be an octave or so shorter.

The harp glissando is most effective when used to add colour and excitement to an upward rush on strings, woodwind, or both together. A diatonic-scale glissando goes very well with a chromatic scale on the wind, no discrepancy between them being discernible to the ear.

The 'splash' effect of a harp glissando is much enhanced by the addition of a stroke or roll on the cymbals with a soft stick.

The student must be careful to avoid the temptation of using the harp glissando to excess. Some harp parts consist almost entirely of zig-zag lines! The late Sir Charles Stanford used to complain that some composers seemed to imagine that harpists played with brooms instead of fingers. Harp parts should consist mainly of well-placed chords and arpeggio-figures. Arpeggios sound best when placed in the middle and upper reaches of the instrument (but not right at the very top).

Harp-harmonics are produced by 'stopping' a string at its middle point with the lower part of the hand and plucking the top half of the string with the fingers. They produce the octave above the natural note of the string and are indicated by the sign O placed above the note. They are only effective in this part of the instrument's compass:

They may be used in both hands simultaneously, and chords of two or three notes can be played by the *left hand* in harmonics if the notes lie close together. Single-note harmonics only can be played by the right hand.

These harmonics have the sound of a very clear and distant bell. They are very easily obscured, and should only be used in conjunction with the *pp* of other instruments, and even then should be marked *mf* at least, if they are to 'tell'. The student should look out for them and make a mental note of their fascinating and beautiful effect.

Their production requires careful adjustment on the part of the player. It is therefore out of the question to write any but very slow passages in harmonics for the harp. Two harps are sometimes used in the orchestra. By setting them to different scales harmonic progressions which would be unplayable on a single harp are made possible. In addition to this great advantage much intricacy of figuration can be devised, and very full and rich chordal writing can be indulged in. Two harps should never be used merely to double each other in unison. It is better to use only one harp unless there is something really helpful and effective for the second harp to do.

One last word with regard to the harp. When a passage lies in an extreme sharp key for the orchestra (e.g. B or F♯) write your harp part in the enharmonically equivalent key (C♭ or G♭). The strings are more resonant when not 'stopped' by the pedals. The same thing applies to isolated notes, 'picked out' by the harp. These ring out with greater clearness when played on 'open' strings.

The Glockenspiel.

In this instrument the sound is produced by striking resonant little metal

bars. Its compass is: (sounding 2 octaves higher).

It possesses a complete chromatic scale between these two notes, and is non-transposing. Its clear tone, like fairy bells, is very attractive. Isolated notes, simple melodic figures, or bell-like *ostinati* suit it well.

78

The Xylophone.

This instrument consists of a series of wooden bars which, when struck, produce notes of definite pitch.

Its compass is [musical notation] (sounding as written).

It is non-transposing and possesses a complete chromatic scale. Its dry 'chippy' tone goes well in association with *pizzicato* or *col legno* strings, and adds extra bite to the muted brass. It is extremely agile, and is especially suited to short rapid passages (containing, for preference, quick repeated notes) in which a hard, expressionless, tone-quality is desirable.

The Celesta.

This instrument possesses a keyboard similar to that of the pianoforte, by means of which hammers are caused to strike steel bars.

Its compass is [musical notation] (sounding an octave higher).

Music for the celesta is written on two staves like that for the piano-forte. It has a complete chromatic scale.

The tone of the celesta is very clear, and much rounder and less tinkling than that of the glockenspiel. It is sometimes used for solo work of a very light and airy character, but is more often used to 'touch in' little phrases, or as a gilt-edging to quiet orchestral ensembles in music of an elegantly fanciful character. Arpeggios suit it well, also glittering chordal writing. Its tone dies away rapidly, but is by no means dry and detached. Single notes or octaves ring out with a kind of starry brilliance. They always suggest to the present writer the taste of a ripe plum. The celesta is incapable of forceful delivery, but its cool clear limpid, yet luscious notes add a feeling of opulence and luxury even to music of a thoroughly commonplace cast.

79

EXERCISES

1. (*a*) Rewrite the following passages for harp in such a way as to involve the fewest possible pedal-changes. Indicate the 'setting' of the strings necessary for each example.

2. Show how the strings of the harp would have to be set to produce the following as glissandos.

(i) Dominant 7th in key of A.

(ii) Dominant 7th in key of D♭.

(iii) Diminished 7th in key of E.

(iv) 'Leading 7th' in key of E♭.

(v) Secondary 7th in key of A♭, on the supertonic.

(vi) 'Added 6th' in key of G♭ (i.e. on subdominant).

CHAPTER IX

THE FULL ORCHESTRAL TUTTI

BEFORE proceeding to consider the treatment of the full orchestra it will be necessary to study the question of balance between the woodwind and brass groups.

The woodwind owing to its vastly inferior volume of tone, when compared with the brass, cannot hope to compete with it, but if used with knowledge and skill it can add considerably to its brilliance and sonority. We are here speaking of ranges of force of *mf* and upwards. In the *p* and *pp* problems of balance do not much arise, as all the instruments are playing with subdued tone. The strings, thanks to their numerical superiority, are able to hold their own against the brass far more successfully than can the woodwind.

In laying out passages for woodwind and brass care should be taken that no essential notes of the harmony are omitted from the brass group. The woodwind can only be used for doubling notes which are already present in the brass. Unison doublings do not help much, if at all, except in the case of high trumpet parts being doubled in unison by clarinets to give steadiness and confidence to the trumpets rather than for any definitely musical result (e.g. clarinets have been used with great success to double the extremely high trumpet parts to be found in the works of Bach and Handel). The clarinets *qua* clarinets are not heard, but they certainly improve the tone of the high trumpets by giving it a rounder, smoother, and more effortless quality.) Eighteenth-century trumpet parts were written very high because of the impossibility of obtaining scale-wise passages on the natural instrument except amongst the very high harmonics of the series. Much light is thrown on this matter by Schweitzer in his *J. S. Bach* (vol. ii, p. 435 et seq.).

The flutes and clarinets, as we know, gain in strength and penetrating power as they ascend, whilst the tone of the oboes becomes thin and impoverished above about B♭ above the treble staff. The bassoons are at their most powerful in their bottom octave or so.

To get the most brilliant tone, then, out of a combination of woodwind and brass, the flutes and clarinets must be placed high (but the clarinets rarely higher than G in alt.), the oboes in their medium, and the bassoons in their bottom register. The large gap between the bassoons and the next woodwind part above is filled by the brass.

If there is no tuba, the part which would have been given to it will be allotted to two bassoons in unison (if it does not go too low for them, of course).

Below is a simple illustration of this, given on two staves to save space. It is the opening of a Trauermarsch by Schubert (for pianoforte, four hands):

The five octaves, from top to bottom, we will call *a*, *b*, *c*, *d*, *e*, and the scoring suggested (which the student should copy out in open score for greater clearness) is as follows:

(*a*) 2 fl. and 2 clar.

(*b*) 2 ob. and 2 trumpets.

(*c*) 1st and 3rd hns., 2 tenor troms.

(*d*) 2nd and 4th hns., bass trom.

(*e*) 2 bassoons (and tuba, if any).

Tschaikovsky in his tuttis (which may be recommended for close study, being models of clearness and sonority) frequently doubles his trumpets at the unison with the oboes. This procedure adds bite and edge to the trumpet tone without in any way detracting from its powerful and impressive quality.

Bassoons, on the other hand, when used in unison with trombones tend to dull their brilliance. They add considerably to the tone of the tuba, however, when used on their low notes.

The double bassoon acts as an excellent 'double bass' to the brass in the *p* and *pp* when used alone. In the *f* and *ff* it helps the tuba to combine with the trombones by imparting to it the 'edge' which it otherwise lacks.

We have already pointed out that clarinets in unison with high trumpets give them increased roundness of tone and certainty of attack. When placed high above the brass (as in the Schubert example above) they reinforce the upper partials, and thus add great brilliance to the ensemble.

The flutes and piccolo act in the same way at still higher altitudes.

Oboes and/or cor anglais add greatly to the nasal tang of hard-blown muted brass, and low 'chalumeau' clarinets and/or bass clarinet combine well in unison with muted horns or trombones at all dynamic levels, but more particularly, perhaps, in the *p* and *pp*.

Strings, Woodwind, and Brass combined.

The lay-out of the tutti of the full orchestra varies much, it is almost needless to say, with the type of music to be orchestrated. The passage for instance might be in the nature of one of the following:

(1) A homogeneous chordal passage.
(2) A powerful melodic line on the top, with simple chords, sustained or detached, below it.
(3) A powerful melodic line in the middle of the orchestral mass with accompanying chords or figures above and below it, sustained or detached.
(4) A powerful melodic line in the bass with accompanying chords or figures above it.
(5) Two melodic lines simultaneously with accompanying chords or figures.
(6) An entirely polyphonic passage (such as might occur in an orchestral fugue, for instance).

One fact should be firmly grasped with regard to the tutti, and that is that the simpler its musical structure is, the more telling and sonorous will be its effect. There should be no waste notes anywhere. Every instrument, however unimportant it may seem, must play a definite part in reinforcing the main lines of the texture. It is worse than useless to overload the score with decorations for the sake of giving the instruments 'something to do'. Such a score may look very clever and knowing to the uninitiated, but the result in performance is a jumble of sound

83

and a blurring of the essential outlines. It must not be forgotten that independent parts given to the feebler instruments are not actually heard in the tutti, but may play havoc with the clarity of design which should be the orchestrator's first aim. Much doubling, therefore, is necessary in the tutti.

We will now take each of the above six alternatives in turn.

(1) A homogeneous chordal passage, such as the following:

In a case like this the best plan, to ensure a solid and uniform body of tone, is to give to each orchestral group—strings, woodwind, and brass—the complete harmony.

The three upper parts of the harmony may be reduplicated at the octave above, and the bass at the octave below. The bass must never be doubled in the *higher* octave. Dire harmonic confusion would result were the bass to be mingled with the upper parts.

Each group, then, must sound complete if played without the others, and the part-writing must in each case be smooth and correct. However, there may—in fact there should—be a large gap between the upper woodwind and the bassoons in accordance with the remarks made on this subject earlier in this chapter.

It will be best to distribute the strings evenly throughout the texture by writing them in extended harmony (with occasional double-stops when these are easily manageable).

The two trumpets and three trombones give us five parts, but we have no intention of spoiling the harmonic clearness by writing a fifth 'real part' for one of these. The tune can, of course, always bear strengthening, and this can be done either by giving it to the two trumpets in unison, and the alto and tenor parts to the tenor trombones, or by giving the alto and tenor parts to the 2nd trumpet and 1st trombone respectively and doubling the tune in the lower octave on the 2nd trombone. The latter alternative is possible here since it does not result in crossing the tune with the bass. We have adopted it because it gives greater strength and dignity and fullness to the design.

The four horns will be well employed if the 1st and 3rd double the two trumpets and the 2nd and 4th the two tenor trombones. The bass trombone and tuba play the bass in octaves. The timpani, tuned to A and E, can play throughout.

This gives the following orchestration, which the student should copy out into full score with the proper transpositions:

Ex. XXVII

The woodwind parts (marked *a, b, c*) would be arranged thus:

   (*a*) Fls. I and II, clar. I (picc. 8va).

   (*b*) Ob. I, clar. II.

   (*c*) Ob. II (+cor anglais).

Note how the horns, in the final chord, *complete* the harmony of the rest of the brass where it threatens to sound thin, having *doubled* it up to that point.

Our next example, taken from the opening of Beethoven's 'Hammer-clavier' Sonata, Op. 106, shows a very different kind of chordal passage:

The first point to be noticed here is the effect of the pedal. The B♭ in the bass must be tied over and held throughout the following bar in our transcription if it is to convey faithfully the composer's intention.

The second point is the distance apart of the two hands. This gap must of course be filled in our score, otherwise it will sound very thin and unsatisfactory.

In our arrangement we have used the strings *pizzicati*. This arrangement gives tremendous rhythmical force and point to full chords of this kind on the wind and brass, especially when chords of three notes are given to each string group (except of course, the double basses). If there were no tuba in the score, the double basses would be used *col arco* to help sustain the pedal B♭, but with the tuba (and also, possibly the double bassoon) present, they are better employed *pizzicati* to support the rest of the strings. Note that only crotchet rhythm is given to the strings. The quaver would be far too quick for the *pizzicato*, especially in chord work like this. The harp, if used, would play big chords (sec) with the strings.

Ex. XXVIII, and the following examples in short score, should be copied out into full score with the proper clefs and transpositions. (The cor anglais, if any, would double the 1st horn in unison. The woodwind parts are too high for it to double effectively.)

(2) Treatment of a powerful melodic line on the top, with simple chords, sustained or detached, below it.

Schubert's pianoforte sonata, **Op. 143**, 1st movement, bars 34–44, furnishes a good example for our purpose:

The passage continues similarly for nine more bars. (How magnificent it is! In its tragic grandeur it seems to forestall by a century some of the finest thoughts of Sibelius.)

The melodic line must stand out with the greatest power and clarity in our arrangement, and obviously calls for a great sweep of strings. The chords in the left-hand part can be extended upwards, and thus enlarged and enriched so as to be suitable for the whole of the brass. To reproduce the slurring of the chords on to the octave D on the 3rd beat of each bar—a pianistic effect—the chords must be tied over to a quaver on the 3rd

beat, the bassoons, tuba, double bass (*pizz.*), timpani, and bass drum
supplying the octave D's.

The woodwind (with the exception of the bassoons) is used to reinforce
the string melody. We have divided the 'cellos in order to obtain
intensity of tone from their high register. Half the 'cellos, however, are
retained for use in the bottom octave of the melody, doubling the violas,
to maintain a proper balance. Questions of balance also determine that
more woodwind shall double the top line (*a*) than (*b*) and (*c*) in this case.
The melody is arranged in three octaves instead of two, for greater
breadth and sonority.

Ex. XXIX

Melodic line
(Strings & Woodwind)

Bassoons & Horns

Trumpets &
Tenor Trombones

Bass Trombone & Tuba
(D. Bass pizz. and
C-Fag. with Tuba)

Timp. in D
(with Bass Dr.)

The three octaves of the melodic line are distributed thus:

   (*a*) Vln. I, 2 fl., ob. I, clar. I.

   (*b*) Vln. II, 1st half of vcl., ob. II (and cor ang.).

   (*c*) Vla., 2nd half of vcl., clar. II (and bass clar.).

The dotted slurs show the bowing for the strings. The wind would play
the passage with the original slurring.

If the melodic line were confined to two octaves with *all* the violins on the top octave and the violas and 'cellos in unison on the lower octave, no woodwind doubling of the strings would be necessary, and the woodwind would then be used to double the brass chords. We are inclined to favour the arrangement we have given, however, for the sake of the added depth and breadth given to the melodic combination by the addition of the lower octave, and the pure brass tone-colour of the chords.

When the accompanying chords are detached, it is not necessary to make the melodic line quite so powerful as it has to be to come through a mass of sustained harmony. 1st and 2nd violins in octaves, doubled by the higher woodwind, should be quite sufficient to carry the melodic line successfully against detached chords on the rest of the orchestra, especially if the brass were marked f and everything else ff.

A few other very powerful melodic combinations possible in the kind of passage we are here considering are:

(i) Top octave: 1st and 2nd violins+fls. and clars. Lower octave: 2 trumpets+oboes.

(ii) Top octave: 2 trumpets. Lower octave: 2 or 3 trombones, or 4 horns.

(iii) Violas, 1 trumpet and all the upper woodwind. The whole in *unison*, not octaves.

(iv) The instruments in (iii) on the upper octave, 'cellos and 4 horns on the lower.

Many other possibilities will suggest themselves. The student must develop his orchestral sense and instinct to enable him to determine what combination is most suitable to the matter in hand.

(3) The third of our six types of tutti concerns the treatment of a powerful melodic line in the middle of the orchestral mass.

Our example comes from a pianoforte duet by Dvorák, 'Aus stürmischen Zeiten', No. 6 of a set of pieces called 'Aus dem Böhmer Walde'. We give the first two bars of the passage, which continues in an exactly similar manner for twelve more bars or so.

It consists of a strongly marked tune in the tenor register with broken chord-patterns above it and an emphatically rhythmical bass.

The most obvious way of laying out this passage would be to give the tune to the trombones (all three in unison), and to distribute the accompanying figures among the rest of the orchestra. The enormous power of the trombones will bring the tune through the whole of the rest of the orchestra, trumpets, percussion, and all, so that the most important problem of balance is immediately solved.

More brilliance still would be given to the tune if the trumpets doubled the trombone at the octave above. This procedure would bring the tune to the foreground without the necessity of blaring on the part of the brass. It is therefore to be recommended, especially as the bass trombone could then be dropped out with safety, and could supply the E and F in the second bar below the tune (and similar harmonic parts in the succeeding bars not given here). Note the way in which the accompanying chords have been amplified in our arrangement. The general lay-out of such a passage is perfectly simple because the tune fits the trumpets and trombones like a glove and they can be trusted to 'come through' anything.

The great thing, as we have said above, and will probably say again, is not to fritter away any of the instruments on parts not essential to the design. Every instrument here is adding what weight it has to one of the four component parts of the texture (*i.e.* ♩♩♩, ♩ 𝄽♩, ♩ 𝄾 ♪ and the tune itself).

90

Ex. XXX

Fl. Clar.

Ob. (Cor Ang.)

Horns (actual sounds)

Trumpets

Troms.

Vln. I, II Violas

Vcl., D-B, Fag, Tuba, (B.Clar.& C-F.)

Timp. D, A

Cym B. D.

Our next example is not quite so simple because the inner part is completely unsuitable for trombones or trumpets.

We have, therefore, to find some combination of instruments which will be sufficiently powerful to penetrate the mass of tone above and below, and, at the same time, leave enough instruments to cope success-

Ex. XXXI

G. J.

Allegro

fully with the rest of the design. This inner part does not go below fiddle G, so that the violins could lend the powerful aid of their G strings to it (coupled with other instruments of course) were it not for the fact that their presence is urgently required to help out the top line. The violas can be used, however, also the 'cellos if they can be spared from the energetic bass part. The trumpets and trombones are, as we have said, ruled out by the nature of the passage, but not so the horns. They can readily manage a passage like this, shake and all, especially if they are well doubled. We will therefore use the four horns in unison. This combination of violas, 'cellos, and four horns would be sufficient to bring the part through, but further breadth and sonority would be gained by the addition of some of the lower woodwind if they can be spared. The bassoons will no doubt be wanted to help the bass line, and the clarinets the top line (which consists, observe, of chords, not just a single line). The cor anglais can probably be spared (if we are using one) but the bass clarinet will be needed for strengthening the bass line, especially as the 'cellos have been taken away from it. We thus have violas, 'cellos, cor anglais, and four horns for our middle line; violins, flutes, oboes, clarinets, and trumpets for the top part of the structure; double basses, bassoons, double bassoon, bass clarinet, tuba, and trombones for the bass line. Passages like this bass part have to be carefully shared between the three trombones in some such way as this:

The three trombones are therefore only equal to one, and the bass line is thus not so heavy as would appear from the list of instruments employed on it. The tuba can play the whole passage as it stands in the original (in the bottom octave, of course). The student should now score the passage for himself on the lines indicated.

(4) Treatment of a principal melodic line in the bass.

Enough has been said with regard to the bass line in the preceding example to indicate the kind of procedure suitable in cases of this kind.

92

Where there is no important inner melodic line the 'cellos are of course available for the bass part, also the violas and horns when the *tessitura* does not lie too low for them. The trombones should only be used for such bass parts as suit them well. Otherwise they are better employed in filling in the middle of the harmony, or in emphasizing salient points by means of their powerful *sforzato*. They are often used to outline a bass part which is being played in its entirety by the more agile bass instruments, e.g.:

This might be scored thus:

Ex. XXXII

The trombones, &c. give the outline only here. The woodwind could, no doubt, manage the passage in its original form, but would be much steadier and would produce far more tone in the above arrangement. The upper octave of the passage is divided between the two pairs of horns, it being impossible to maintain such rapid tonguing for more than a very short time. Their part is marked staccato to ensure the clear articulation of every note.

For a melodic bass line, then, we have the following instruments available:

Strings. 'Cellos and double basses (and violas).
Woodwind. Bassoons, double bassoon, bass clar. (and clarinets).

93

Brass. Tuba (and horns and/or trombones).

The instruments given in brackets are not always available, either owing to lack of necessary depth, or unsuitability to the particular matter in hand.

(5) Two melodic lines of equal strength simultaneously, with accompanying chords or figures.

The two melodic lines may occur in the following ways:

(*a*) In the extreme parts (top line and bottom line).

(*b*) In the top part and an inner part well removed from it in pitch.

(*c*) In the bass and an inner part.

Case (*a*) need not detain us. We have already studied the treatment of melodic lines in treble and bass separately. It should therefore be a matter of no difficulty to combine them.

(*b*) The equal balancing of the two melodic lines in this case, and, at the same time, making them sufficiently powerful to come through the orchestral tutti, presents little difficulty if the simple principles of doubling are well understood and applied. It is desirable, in addition, to contrast the instrumental colour of the two lines, that is to say, not to be content with using two sets of exactly similar instruments for the two melodic lines. This is an easy way of obtaining equal balance, but is weak and unresourceful and musically unsatisfying.

E.g.   Top line: Vln. I, ob. I, clar. I, trumpet I.

Lower line: Vln. II, ob. II, clar. II, trumpet II (or trombone).

This is dull and uninteresting in the extreme. Cases might occur, however, such as the following, taken from Arthur Benjamin's Piano Suite,[1] which seem to demand brass tone in both lines from the nature of the tune itself.

With swinging rhythm

[1] Oxford University Press.

THE FULL ORCHESTRAL TUTTI

Even so it would be better to arrange it thus:

(a) 2 trumpets		(a) 2 trumpets
	than	
(b) 4 horns		(b) 2 trombones

owing to the contrast between the 'edge-tone' of the trumpets and the rounder tone of the horns. The actual *balance* is the same, as we know, in both cases.

The following are suggestions for equal balance and contrasted tone-colours in the tutti between melodic lines in general (not necessarily only applicable to the example above) occurring respectively in the 'soprano' and 'tenor' registers. The doublings are at the unison, not the octave.

1. (a) Vlns. I and II, fls., and clar. I.
   (b) Vla., vcl., cor ang., and clar. II (or bass clar.).
2. (a) Vlns. I and II and vlas.
   (b) Clars., fags., cor ang., bass clar., and 2 horns.
3. (a) Vlas., 1 trumpet, fls., and obs.
   (b) 'Cellos, 2 horns, clars., and fags.

No. 2 shows strings only on the top line and wind only on the lower line.

Other similar combinations will occur to the student who has absorbed the principles of balance. Care must be taken, of course, not to use up too many instruments for the two melodic lines so that insufficient remain to deal with the accompanying musical texture.

(c) Melodic lines in an inner part and the bass.

Similar considerations as to balance and colour contrast hold good here. Here are a few ideas of how the two lines might be arranged, (e) representing the inner ('alto' or 'tenor') part and (f) the bass.

(N.B. (e) represents a unison combination, (f) an octave combination.)

1. (e) Vlns. I and II (G string), 2 horns (cor ang.), 2 clars.
   (f) Vcl. and D. B, 2 fags. (bass clar. and C fag.), tuba.
2. (e) Vla., Vcl., 4 horns.
   (f) D. B, 3 troms., tuba, 2 fags. (bass clar. and C fag.).
3. (e) 2 troms. (or 3, if pitch permits of use of bass trom.).
   (f) Vcl., D. B, 2 fags., horns II and IV, tuba.

(6) Lastly we have to consider a tutti in which the music is purely polyphonic.

Our example consists of the final stretto of the five-part B♭ minor fugue (No. 22, Bk. I, of Bach's '48').

In scoring this magnificent stretto the two most important considerations are:

(1) To ensure that each entry is well defined and emphasized.
(2) To arrange things so that every 'voice', after having entered, is of approximately the same strength as every other.

In orchestrating fugues, and polyphonic music in general, there should be no octave-doubling of inner parts where such doubling would cause crossing of parts which would result in harmonic confusion. The top and bottom parts may, however, be doubled at the higher and lower octave respectively.

When working this example the writer first made sure of good balance in the *brass* department. After that the strings were added, one part to each of the five 'voices', the 1st violins an octave higher than in the original and the double basses an octave lower. The woodwind double the brass and string parts. The manner in which they do this should be carefully observed.

The student should also note the way in which consideration (1) referred to above has been carried out.

96

Ex. XXXIII

EXERCISES

Arrange the following passages for full orchestral tutti:

1. Any chorale or hymn-tune.
2. Brahms, Rhapsody in E♭, Op. 119, No. 4, bars 1–64.[1]
3. Grieg, 'Auf den Bergen' (No. 1 of 'Aus dem Volksleben', Op. 19), bars 99–126.
4. Brahms, Ballad in D minor, Op. 10, No. 1, bars 27–48.
5. Chopin, Polonaise in C minor, Op. No. 2, the last 17 bars.
6. Bach, Fugue in D minor (from Chromatic Fantasia and Fugue), the last 22 bars.
7. Schumann, 'Carnaval', bars 1–25 of the 'Préambule'.

[1] Of course all the instruments will not play all the time in this passage, but it calls for heavy scoring throughout, and is therefore classed as a 'tutti'.

CHAPTER X

GENERAL REMARKS

THE student should now be in a position to attempt the orchestration of complete movements for full orchestra. We have endeavoured in the foregoing chapters to indicate how some of the problems of scoring and arranging may be met and overcome. Every piece of music will be found to present its own problems, and it is manifestly impossible to give formulae whereby an infinite number of contingencies may be dealt with. As in composition so in orchestration it is only the technique of the subject which can be learned from books or from teachers. The application of this technique depends entirely upon the extent of the musicianship, inventiveness, experience, and general sense of appropriateness with which the individual is naturally endowed.

A few words of warning designed to guard the beginner against the most common faults may, however, be of use:

(1) Avoid the 'sectional' effect produced by constantly using contrasted groups of instruments in turn, e.g. a section for strings alone followed by one for woodwind alone, then by one for brass, then strings alone again. This may occasionally be done if the character of the music demands it, but generally speaking a blending or fusion of the various groups with one another makes for continuity and homogeneity. Organists might compare the sectional method with that of the constant contrast of great, swell, and choir organs. The music never seems to 'get going' when this is indulged in to excess.

(2) Avoid thickness. This is caused by too low and 'grumpy' placing of the harmony. 'Open' harmonic spacing is desirable in the lower registers of the orchestra. It may also be caused by the desire to give some instrument or group of instruments something to do. Do not have instruments meandering pointlessly about in the score. They obscure the outlines of the music and if not required to give point or weight to some part of the texture they had far better be given rests.

(3) Avoid thinness. This has been insisted upon throughout the book. Wide spaces between the bass and the next part above it should only be allowed as a special and calculated effect. Holding notes on a single

horn are often sufficient to fill such gaps, and give stability and body to the structure.

(4) Do not regard the brass and drums solely as noise-makers. They may frequently be used *pp* with excellent effect.

(5) Do not keep your horns going all the time. There is a great tendency amongst beginners to do this. A warm 'wad' of horns is bound to prevent thinness in the middle octaves of the orchestra, but their continuous use palls on the ear and tires the players.

(6) Reserve extreme high notes on woodwind and brass for *fff* climaxes, and be sparing of them even then.

(7) Remember that the strings are the foundation of the orchestra, and do not be afraid to use them alone for quite long passages if you wish to do so. The ear does not quickly tire of string-tone which is the most beautiful and variable of all orchestral sounds. In quiet passages use 'divisi' rather than double-stops. In passages of a more forceful nature double-stops are often desirable, especially in the 2nd violins and violas. Make sure that they are easy to play.

(8) In scoring song-accompaniments the first necessity is, of course, to let the voice through. High notes, especially on open vowels, will be heard clearly above the forte of strings, woodwind, and horns if nothing is placed higher than the voice. (Men's voices count, for this purpose, as though they were sounding an octave above their true pitch.) Low notes on all voices are covered up by low oboes, clarinets, and bassoons. The safest rule for the inexperienced scorer is to rely mainly on the strings for his accompaniments, and to keep the dynamic markings of the wind at a low level. Pianissimo brass chords form an effective background to the baritone or bass voice in solemn declamatory passages, provided that the voice is being employed in its medium or upper registers. Otherwise it is safer to reserve the brass for the interludes and *ritornelli*, or for passages in which the vocal phrases are punctuated by detached chords for full orchestra. Extreme restraint must always be observed in accompanying the voice. In the theatre it is not necessary to keep the orchestra under to quite the extent required in the concert-hall, owing to the fact that the tones of the orchestra are somewhat damped and muffled in the theatre band-pit, but even here it is far wiser to err on the side of too slight rather than too full accompaniment.

100

In accompanying choral music, the chorus, if it be of reasonable dimensions, can hold its own against, and even swamp, the full orchestra. The aim here must therefore be to give solid support to the chorus, and to lay on the colour in bold splashes. Only in the quiet passages can orchestral subtleties make their effect. Those who wish to make a special study of choral accompaniment are advised to consult Cecil Forsyth's admirably sane and practical work, *Choral Orchestration* (Novello & Co. Ltd.).

Finally, hear as much orchestral music as you can, and study closely as many scores as you can beg, borrow, or buy.

In connexion with the study of scores it will be found most instructive and helpful to make arrangements, from the full score, for pianoforte (solo or duet) or organ, of movements from standard orchestral works, also to rescore movements from pianoforte duet arrangements, for the orchestra for which they were originally written, and afterwards to compare your scoring with the original full score.

EXERCISES

Score the following:[1]

1. Schubert, Sonata in A minor, Op. 42. First movement.
2. Chopin, Polonaise in A major, Op. 40, No. 1.
3. Mendelssohn, Scherzo in E minor, Op. 16, No. 2.
4. Mendelssohn, Fugue in E minor, Op. 35, No. 1.
5. Beethoven, Sonata in A♭, Op. 26. Finale.
6. Grieg, Sonata in E minor, Op. 7. Finale.
7. Debussy, 'La Soirée dans Grenade' (from Estampes).
8. Debussy, 'La Cathédrale Engloutie'.
9. Moussorgsky, 'La cabane sur les pattes de poule', 'Les Bohatyrs de Kiew'. Tableaux d'une exposition.
10. Brahms, Variations and Fugue on a Theme of Handel, Op. 24.

The following exercises are suggested as aids to the study of scores in general:

I. Arrange the following for pianoforte (preferably four hands):
  1. Mozart, G minor Symphony. First movement.
  2. Beethoven, Symphony No. 2 in D. Slow movement.

[1] For further exercises see Appendix overleaf.

3. Wagner, Siegfried Idyll.
4. Tschaikovsky, Movements from the Casse-Noisette Suite.
5. Wagner, Prelude to 'Tristan und Isolde'.
6. Debussy, 'Prélude à l'après-midi d'un faune'.

II. Arrange the following for organ:

1. Beethoven, Slow movement ('Marche Funèbre') from Symphony No. 3 (Eroica).
2. Mendelssohn, 'Hebrides' Overture.
3. Schubert, Symphony in B minor (the Unfinished).
4. Wagner, 'Meistersinger' Overture.
5. Tschaikovsky, Slow movement from Symphony No. 5.

III. Score the following from pianoforte duet arrangements using in each case exactly the orchestra for which they were originally written. Afterwards compare your score with the original. Use natural horns and trumpets for the Mozart, Beethoven, and Schubert examples.

1. Mozart, Symphony in E flat. First movement. (Pf. duet published by Augener's.)
2. Beethoven, Symphony No. 7 in A. Slow movement. (Pf. duet published by Augener's.)
3. Schubert, Symphony in C major. Slow movement. (Pf. duet published by Augener's.)
4. Dvořák, 'New World' Symphony. First movement. (Pf. duet published by Simrock.)
5. Tschaikovsky, Symphony No. 6 (Pathétique). Last movement. (Pf. solo published by Augener's.)
6. Elgar, Enigma Variations. (Pf. duet and Full Score published by Novello's.)

All the above full scores may be purchased quite cheaply in miniature editions through Messrs. Hawkes or Messrs. Goodwin & Tabb.

The student would be well advised to acquaint himself with the following masterly transcriptions by means of (1) study of the score, where available, and comparison of it with the original; (2) attending perfor-

GENERAL REMARKS

mances of them at the earliest opportunity; (3) gramophone records, where available:

Brahms, Orchestration of his own St. Antoni Chorale (Haydn), Variations. Originally written for two pianos. (Score from Goodwin & Tabb).

Berlioz, 'Invitation to the Waltz'. Weber.

Elgar, Fantasia and Fugue in C minor. Bach. (Novello.)
    Overture in D minor. Handel. (Novello.)

Henri Busser, Petite Suite. Debussy.

Ravel, 'Pictures from an Exhibition'. Moussorgsky.

Henry J. Wood, 'Pictures from an Exhibition'. Moussorgsky. (Superior to Ravel's in picturesqueness and vividness.)

Weingartner, 'Invitation to the Waltz'. Weber.
    'Hammerclavier' Sonata. Beethoven. (Breitkopf & Härtel.)

Klenovsky, Toccata and Fugue in D minor. Bach. (O.U.P.)

Ravel, Orchestration of his own Suites 'Ma mère L'oye' and 'Le tombeau de Couperin'.

Anthony Collins, Grand Duo in C. Schubert.

Hamilton Harty, 'A John Field Suite'.

APPENDIX

FURTHER SUGGESTIONS FOR EXERCISES IN ORCHESTRATION

The Small Orchestra (as in Chapter V).

1. Tschaikovsky, 'Feuillet d'album', Op. 19, No. 3.
2. Mendelssohn, Scherzo à Capriccio in F♯ mi. (without Op. No.).
3. Chopin, Nocturne in B major, Op. 32, No. 1.
4. Ireland, 'The Towing Path'.
5. Ireland, 'The Darkened Valley'.
6. Grieg, 'Poetic Tone-pictures', Op. 3, Nos. 1, 5, and 6.

A Theatre Orchestra.

One flute (changing with piccolo), one oboe, two clarinets, one bassoon,

103

two horns, two trumpets, one tenor trombone, timpani and percussion (one player), harp, and strings.

1. Chopin, 'Grande Valse Brillante', Op. 18.
2. Tschaikovsky, 'Mazurka de Salon', Op. 9, No. 3.
3. Mendelssohn, 7 characteristic pieces, Op. 7, No. 4.
4. Tschaikovsky, 'En Traineau', Op. 37, No. 11.
5. Grieg, 'Norwegian Bridal Procession', Op. 19, No. 2.
6. Albeniz, 'Tango', Op. 165, No. 2.
7. Albeniz, 'Malagueña' (Rumores de la Caleta, No. 6).

The Full Orchestra.

1. Mendelssohn, Fugue in E minor, without Op. No. (Augener's Edn. No. 5074).
2. Dvořák, 'Aus stürmischen Zeiten' (No. 6 of 'Aus dem Böhmer Walde') for piano duet, Op. 68.
3. Schumann, 'Carnaval'; all numbers are suitable except the piece named 'Paganini'.
4. Beethoven, Sonata in E♭, Op. 81a, 1st movement ('Les Adieux').
5. Bach, Prelude and Fugue in G minor from Book II of the '48'.
6. Schubert, Many marches and other pieces for piano duet.
7. Schubert, Waltzes. (Numerous, and mostly suitable.)
8. Chabrier, 'Pièces pittoresques'.
9. Bartók, 15 Hungarian Folk-songs.
10. Bax, 'In a Vodka Shop'.
11. Ireland, 'Ragamuffin'.
12. Bartók, 'Allegro barbaro'.
13. Albeniz, 'Iberia'.
14. Albeniz, 'Seguidillas' (Rumores de la Caleta, No. 5).

INDEX

NOTES

NOTES

NOTES

NOTES

NOTES

NOTES

NOTES

NOTES